ENDORSEMENTS

I've worked with Niccie for years, and love how passionate she is about sharing 'The Good News' with others to transform homes, communities, and ultimately the nation. *Kairos Time*, written by Angela Crist, Barb Miller, and Niccie Kliegl teaches women how to fervently pursue freedom from a difficult past, to embrace their inner beauty as God does, and to step into the call God has on their life.

—Shemane Nugent,
Lifestyle and Healthy Living Expert

Kairos Time gives us many profound and powerful examples of redemption. It should be a textbook for the troubled and confused. It's filled with well-written stories of painful seasons and charged with permission to hope again.

—Ray Hughes, founder of Selah Ministries, international speaker, prophet, author, storyteller, singer/songwriter, and musicologist

KAIROS TIME

BURNING OFF THE PAST
LIGHTING UP THE PRESENT
BLAZING INTO THE FUTURE

KAIROS TIME

BURNING OFF THE PAST
LIGHTING UP THE PRESENT
BLAZING INTO THE FUTURE

Angela Crist
Barb Miller
Niccie Kliegl

Kairos Time © 2021
by Angela Crist, Barb Miller, and Niccie Kliegl.
All rights reserved.

Printed in the United States of America

Published by Author Academy Elite
PO Box 43, Powell, OH 43065
www.AuthorAcademyElite.com

All rights reserved. This book contains material protected under International and Federal Copyright Laws and Treaties. Any unauthorized reprint or use of this material is prohibited. No part of this book may be reproduced or transmitted in any form or by any means, electronic or mechanical, including photocopying, recording, or by any information storage and retrieval system, without express written permission from the author.

Library of Congress Control Number: 2021918021

Paperback ISBN: 978-1-64746-889-7
Hardback ISBN: 978-1-64746-890-3
E-book ISBN: 978-1-64746-891-0
Available in paperback, hardback, e-book, and audiobook

All Scripture quotations, unless otherwise indicated, are taken from the Holy Bible, New International Version®, NIV®. Copyright © 1973, 1978, 1984 by Biblica, Inc.™ Used by permission of Zondervan. All rights reserved worldwide.

Any Internet addresses (websites, blogs, etc.) and telephone numbers printed in this book are offered as a resource. They are not intended in any way to be or imply an endorsement by Author Academy Elite, nor does Author Academy Elite vouch for the content of these sites and numbers for the life of this book.

Book design by: JETLAUNCH
Cover design by: Debbie O'Byrne

TABLE OF CONTENTS

ENDORSEMENTS		i
FOREWORD		ix
A NOTE TO THE READER		xi
ACKNOWLEDGEMENTS		xv
KAIROS KICKSTART & ASSESSMENT		xvii
PART 1:	**BURNING OFF THE PAST**	**1**
	CHAPTER ONE	3
	In the Beginning	3
	CHAPTER TWO	18
	Land	18
	CHAPTER THREE	32
	Path	32
	CHAPTER FOUR	44
	Garden	44
	CHAPTER FIVE	59
	Foundation	59
	CHAPTER SIX	71
	Basement	71

PART 2:	**LIGHTING UP THE PRESENT**	**85**
	CHAPTER SEVEN	87
	Recognize	87
	CHAPTER EIGHT	99
	Remove	99
	CHAPTER NINE	110
	Repurpose	110
	CHAPTER TEN	121
	Redeem	121
	CHAPTER ELEVEN	132
	Realize	132
PART 3:	**BLAZING INTO THE FUTURE**	**151**
	CHAPTER TWELVE	153
	Called	153
	CHAPTER THIRTEEN	163
	Ask	163
	CHAPTER FOURTEEN	173
	Seek	173
	CHAPTER FIFTEEN	185
	Knock	185
	CHAPTER SIXTEEN	192
	Activated	192
	MEET THE AUTHORS	200

Foreword

Niccie, Barb, and Angela have masterfully charted a path for readers to move past footholds holding them back from all God has to offer. It begins with stepping out, in expectant faith, toward the work God has called them to while embracing all the wonder and glory that awaits followers of Christ.

In the three parts to this book, each author owns their unique work and process as they lead the reader to a deeper awareness with every chapter for more healing, abundance, and direction.

Igniting Souls Publishing Agency loves to see their books destined for more than an inspiring read. *Kairos Time* is already transforming the hearts, minds, and souls of those who read it. With each chapter, these talented authors have woven in life applications in addition to developing a powerful online course, workshops, and retreats to accompany the teaching.

I'm excited to see how these women and this book will impact the Kingdom.

—Kary Oberbrunner, *Wall Street Journal* and *USA Today* bestselling author, and CEO of Igniting Souls Publishing Agency

A NOTE TO THE READER

Was there a moment in time when everything changed for you? Maybe yours is yet to come. Some can look back and remember a time when they believed they could do all things, and have no idea why now they simply cope, get by, or accept that "dreams are not for everyone." Too often we fall into the trap of believing we are bound to the confines of this crazy world we call home, unable to make huge impacts and impossible-seeming actions.

For many, there is a moment in time when we are robbed of the dreams God put in us. Whether it be slow in coming or in one dreadful act, our identity shifts. At this point, you may suddenly or not so suddenly have forgotten the plans and purposes for your life. Your firewall of protection was compromised. You started believing lies about your value and worth. The enemy of your soul sent in a virus to bring contamination and destruction to your inner workings, your switchboard, your gears, and wheels. You fell out of sync with the frequencies of heaven. Your heart's sound no longer resonated with the melody of an angelic choir but instead partnered with the clamor and gongs of the world.

This new sound created an agreement with a world operated by the king of thieves. This thief fears that someday you will uncover your identity theft and walk in all that you've been called to be. This thief knows that if you uncover his evil tactics, you will be reminded of what was spoken over you before you were ever knit together in your mother's womb. This thief knows that if you uncover the lies he forced you to believe in your most impressionable years, you will destroy his kingdom of darkness.

The only way to bring in a revelation of truth for your life is to invite the Father of Lights into the situation. The One who created the light to begin with. The One who sets your soul on Fire. The One who made you fearfully and wonderfully. The One who serves as an anchor for your soul and removes all the walls so that you may enter into His glory.

The Father of Lights is the original designer of your blueprints. He owns the copyrights to your design and purpose. He roars over your life like a lion. He has released a shout and thunder of your purpose. He has set His eyes of love upon you and He waits patiently for the day that you discover the depth, width, and height of His unconditional love and commitment for you.

He waits.
He's faithful.
He surrounds you.
Always.

He's like a fresh drink in a desert.
He's like a safe place in a storm.
He's like the shade under scorching temperatures.

He's a mighty tower to climb so that your perspective changes. He calls through the darkness with a voice of love. He desires you to climb up, up, UP so that you may set your sights higher and take in a bird's eye view through a heavenly lens.

He's a rock to lean on.
He's your ever-present help in time of need.
And He chases after you.

He watches you as you sleep at night like a mama watches over her precious babe. He watches your chest raise with each breath. He is the creator of those breaths. He loves each breath. They serve as one more day, one more moment, one more opportunity ... to sing His praises, to glorify He who calls you out of darkness and into His marvelous light.

He loves the sound He's given you. You are an intricate part of His symphony. Without your sound, something is missing in the great heavenly orchestra.

He anxiously awaits your sweet smile each morning. He adores your cute little ways. He loves your special personality and sense of humor. He gave them to you. He made you for fellowship and relationship. He made you for connection and intimacy (*in-to-me-u-see*, Lord). He loves when you wake up each day.

He waits by your side as you climb out of bed. He waits to enter your day with you. He's the perfect partner, the seasoned friend, the trustworthy companion, the confidant you've always longed for.

And exactly as we desire a true relationship with our children, He formed you for relationship with Him. He designed you for a purpose to touch His heart so that He may touch yours. This partnership is part of the greatest story ever told. This story is where heaven meets earth. This story is where you gain the privilege of discovering what you were made for. This story is where you remember your purpose so that you may proclaim His excellencies.

Yes friends, there's a place in Him that can only be filled by YOU. Take His hand ... would you please? He's reaching out now.

Let's go . . . *Burn off Your Past.*

Let's courageously . . . *Light up Your Present.*

Let's walk in boldness and . . . *Blaze into Your Future.*

This is your *kairos* moment.

Acknowledgements

We want to thank Ethos, Kary Oberbrunner, CEO of Igniting Souls Publishing, and the whole publishing team. Without you this book would not have been possible.

We also give thanks to each other. Without the loving support of one another, we would be unable to accomplish all God has in store for us. He uniquely designed us with varying gifts and talents that we shared generously in order for the book, all the course content, and community development to be ready for publication, and so powerfully.

All three of us send our deepest gratitude to our families who selflessly edited, encouraged, and picked up the slack while the book was being written.

Lastly, we want to thank our Lord God, the Holy Spirit, and Savior to whom we owe our lives. He is our leader above all, who shows us how to navigate this world and the work we do, successfully. He is the one who first taught us to love graciously, and then to lead according to the Word.

Thank you,

Angela, Barb, and Niccie

KAIROS KICKSTART & ASSESSMENT

The KAIROS ASSESSMENT includes three free 3-DAY TRAINING SESSIONS based on your results.

- **IDENTITY:** An assessment to identify areas that have been holding you back, keeping you from the blessings God has in store for you, and indicate how well you're stepping into your call up to this point.
- **PAST:** Deeper & Higher 3-DAY Mini-course. Find inner healing and life transformation.
- **PRESENT:** God's Design 3-DAY Mini-course. Embrace inner beauty for your home and life.
- **FUTURE:** Praying Power 3-DAY Mini-course. Learn to Tap into the Trinity for life-transforming power.

kairostimecoaching.com

PART 1

Burning off the Past

CHAPTER ONE
IN THE BEGINNING

We'd like to start by getting on the same page, in the same moment of time. *A time that we feel is God-appointed for you and every reader.* A time that will become more than yesterday, today, and tomorrow combined...

Kairos

Throughout this chapter, each author—Angela Crist, author of Part One, Barb Miller, author of Part Two, and Niccie Kliegl, author of Part Three—will share some of their stories with you. They will reference God's perfect timing in their lives, nudging you to become a witness to God's great presence and work-at-hand in your own life, in the here and now.

". . . another word for time is also used in the New Testament—*kairos*. This speaks more to specific, God-ordained times throughout history, sometimes called the 'right time' or 'appointed season' (Titus 1:3). Kairos is God's dimension—one not marked by the past, the present, or the future.

PART 1

"When Jesus came, it was a fulfillment of promises past, a cosmic collision of the sacred and secular. It was an intersection of the holy will of God and the stubborn ways of man. It was a perfect moment. John the Baptist said in Mark 1:15 that 'time is fulfilled, and the kingdom of God is at hand.'

"This godly *kairos* pierced its way into creation at just the right time, slicing through *chronos* with a cry of a baby in a manger.

"The cross was another *kairos* moment. Romans 5:6 says, *'For while we were still helpless, at the right time, Christ died for the ungodly.'*

"*Kairos* moments then—and now—allow us to get a glimpse of the 'other side.' We peek around the corner at eternity. We actually glimpse how God works.

"As the omniscient, omnipresent Deity, God is not bound by the confines of space or time. That's why He flows into our existence when we least expect Him."[1]

We hope this book reveals to you *kairos* times in your life—times where you gain a glimpse of how He has pierced through this busy, distracting, costly world . . . regardless of the stage of your faith journey. We will walk you through three powerful phases in your life: the past, the present, and the future. However, we want you to know the power of **time** over them all, the power of God's timing in them all, and that He is not bound by any of them. And most importantly, His power moving in you from this day forward.

We want to open your eyes to the *kairos* moment of your beautiful creation, of the pivotal moments in your life leading up to your acceptance of Christ, and of the fulfillment that awaits you.

---

[1] Living a Kairos Life in a Chronos World
Blog / Produced by The High Calling
https://www.theologyofwork.org/the-high-calling/blog/living-kairos-life-chronos-world

The God of *kairos* is not bound by space or time. He has appointed us, for the here and now, in preparation of the fulfillment of scripture.

Let's take a walk through time in the lives of your authors, Angela, Barb, and Niccie.

Meet Angela Crist, Author of Part One, Burning off the Past

I was born wildly creative and I always had an imagination higher than the sky. My days were filled with make-believe and it was nothing for me to play out the parts of doctor, mother, teacher, or preacher all in one day. I didn't have limitations or insecurities holding me back. I could be anything because I was made for greatness!

Perhaps my little heart still believed what my spirit always knew before I had been knit together in my mother's womb. Perhaps before I was polluted in my mind and heart, I intimately knew my Heavenly Father. After all, when you know the heart of the Father, you know you are destined to be an overcomer.

When I was five years old, we moved to my grandfather's farm and my life became even more exciting. To add to my imagination, I now had lots of animals to keep me company. I spent my days chasing chickens, feeding baby goats, and dressing cats up in baby-doll clothes. My mind was free and my heart was full of carefree joy. I had the world by the tail and I loved being me.

Then one day, in a flash, my reality changed. A family came to visit us and their teenage son decided to take me to the back woods to play "house." My little innocent mind couldn't quite grasp what was taking place but this I know . . .

That would be the day that the enemy of my heart would impart lies and create for me a new reality.

PART 1

Suddenly, I was oddly aware that Mom was too busy to spend time with me, Dad was unengaged with my heart, and my older siblings didn't want me around anymore. Was this 100% truth? Probably not. But when you are a traumatized child, your ability to process life correctly is skewed. You see things through an immature mind and a tainted lens.

All I know is that from there on out, I didn't feel like I was enough anymore. A new garment was laid over my shoulders. Instead of wearing a superhero cape in rainbow colors, I was now wearing a black cloak that was intricately woven with threads of shame, condemnation, and fear.

Looking in the mirror became painful as well. The enemy had me viewing my head full of lovely curls, my small-framed glasses, and my stocky little body as disgusting, repulsive, and unlovely. This would be my new reality upon which I would start building a foundation. These lies created an ugly weed that would soon grow roots spreading into every area of my life.

Do you have past traumas that have caused you to look through a distorted lens?

As these lies were now cemented in my brain, the enemy of my soul was able to conveniently and wickedly throw at me the perfect scenarios and storms that would only solidify the messages against my heart. Each offense would serve as individual nails driven into my coffin where I would become a corpse—hidden in darkness, disconnected from reality, unable to breathe, and failing to thrive.

I looked to every relationship to fill the aching and gaping wounds of my heart. I bent over backwards to please people; I blindly followed the crowd, didn't have a mind of my own, and was riddled with rejection and insecurity. However, I became a pretty good actress and learned very quickly how to perform and put on a good face, so most would never have known what I was hiding within me.

I knew the Lord as a little girl but as the years went by, He seemed very distant to me. I desperately needed an encounter of His love but instead I continued to seek that love in relationships. In my teenage years I was violated two more times by two more men because I was in the wrong place at the wrong time. And at 18 years old, I married my high school sweetheart. Our relationship was black or white without many gray areas. We had good times and highs but they were far outweighed by the lows.

We were clearly too young to know how to properly steward each other's hearts and our 11 years of marriage were filled with infidelity, fighting, financial heartache, and struggles. We were two broken individuals trying to build a solid life together with no one to disciple our orphan hearts. We did, however, manage to be blessed with three wonderful children in our marriage. God gave us two daughters and a son.

Our marriage ended when my husband left us for another woman. I then found myself in a whirlwind of loneliness and depression. In my desperation to find love, I ended up in some very toxic relationships and was violated twice more by two more men. I was convinced my heart would only be chosen by those who wanted to use me for their own sinful desires. True love existed only in fairytales. I was a moving target for unhealthy predators.

After five years of being single, I finally met the man of my dreams and we married. He became the safe place for my heart to land and after one year of marriage, the Lord decided to put His finger on every wound that had never been healed. Through a series of unfortunate hits from the enemy, I quickly went into a downhill spiral and found myself literally fighting for my life. I fractured out through disassociation from past traumas, had a nervous breakdown, and went into sleep deprivation psychosis.

My sweet hubby managed my heart so well as I spent the next three years walking with the Lord through all of the trauma and disappointments I had never wanted to face before. I learned at that time that our bodies are like huge memory cards and we hang on to trauma at the cellular level. There were times I struggled with suicidal thoughts, and my body

PART 1

would involuntarily shake and quiver as I relived horrendous pain and flashbacks. Healing seemed so far away.

Once I was able to work through all of the trauma, I began to have a real heart for women in ministry. There is no question that the anointing on my life is to be used to set captives free. There is an awakening happening where women are finding their true identity and purpose. We are called to go back and save those wounded warriors who were left for dead (Isaiah 61). These are the ones the enemy threw into ditches and thought no one would ever rescue. I know because I used to be one of them.

My journey of healing literally cost me everything. It cost me friends, family, and my reputation. God used it to shake loose everything that did not look like Him and rebuilt my foundation into an unmovable force for His kingdom assignments. I'm so grateful now that God hand-picked me to walk that hard path. I was called forth to forge through the refiner's fire. The word "chosen" looks different to me now. Before I was chosen for abuse. Now I'm chosen to walk into wholeness and lead others down their paths of restoration.

I currently operate as an ordained apostle and pastor, coach, speaker, and inner healing minister. With the Holy Spirit's leading, I guide people to freedom through the power of Jesus Christ. I literally feel a groaning in my belly for those who do not know who they are and whose they are. Identity is everything! When a person is freed from all the trauma, hurts, and lies against their hearts, they are an unstoppable force for the kingdom of heaven. I love watching people transformed through the love of the Savior.

I am also an entrepreneur in the direct sales industry. My spiritual walk parallels my physical walk. I raise up and mentor warriors who then go on to raise up and mentor other warriors. It is the gift that keeps on giving and it is so rewarding to serve the Lord in this way.

What is your heart's desire? Could it be in ministry?

IN THE BEGINNING

Writing this book has been an absolute privilege and honor, all to the glory of the One who turned my ashes into beauty—He who has allowed me to reach so many through my ministry. However, He has so much more than we could ever imagine in store for us. Allowing Him to open my eyes to all that is in store for His people resulted in a beautiful partnership between myself and my co-authors, whom I adore.

Barb and I met at a very turbulent time in her life. The Lord intricately wove us together, without question. We have powered through many dark times and we have celebrated many spiritual victories. She seems like more of a sister to me than a friend. We have thoroughly enjoyed our "iron sharpens iron" relationship. Her life is a reflection of true beauty and grace and I am so blessed that the Lord has given me a front row seat to witness it all.

Niccie and I met through a mutual author and friend. I hired her as my personal life coach and it didn't take long to recognize the absolute blessing she is to the body of Christ. She is a powerhouse leader who launches people into their destiny and purpose. She has encouraged me, and through her leadership I have been gloriously stretched. I value her friendship.

In my section of the book, my desire is to pinpoint the places in your life where the enemy laid foundational lies and deception that have held you back from being all that you were created to be. My goal is to show you how powerful you are and guide you into a trade out. Together we will exchange your areas of mourning for pure joy.

My approach is a bit different. Instead of teaching, I am going to take you on a journey of self-discovery. You will never look at the outdoors the same way again! My prayer is that you will be able to pick out some land, lay your foundations, and establish your dwelling, in the hope that you will be able to build a house fit for a King.

PART 1

Meet Barb Miller, Author of Part Two, Lighting up the Present

My earliest memories are of coloring—coloring inside the lines with the most beautiful colors and shades from my box of 64 Crayola crayons. This idea of creating something beautiful excited my young heart. As I entered elementary school, my drawings and paintings were often chosen for the hall walls or the upcoming art shows. But I must say, I preferred drawing over painting; it was safer, and more precise. Painting made me uncomfortable because it was . . . well . . . a letting-go of some sort.

You see, I grew up in a conservative home. My parents were kind and loving, but we were definitely not allowed to color "outside" of ANY lines. After all, what would people think? That was an ever-present phrase that was used often in my house, sometimes even out loud, but mostly it rang in our heads. So, I quickly adopted that mindset to guide my young life, along with my list of do's and don'ts. I never left home without it; it was a mental list that I meticulously checked and then double checked. You see, I was the "good girl" always trying to please, always striving to be good enough and to make the right decisions.

Throughout my school years, I was known for my art abilities and creativity. This was fine, but art was never my main focus; it was simply something that came easy. Friends were my thing; I was energized by having them, and lots of them! I was in every sport my parents would allow me to join—not because I was a stellar athlete by any means, but because that's where the action could be found. I spent my high school years either practicing or playing basketball, volleyball, or track, along with being a cheerleader and all the extracurricular activities I could squeeze in between.

As my interests varied, so did my friends. I liked everyone. I know that sounds silly, but I hated to see anyone left out or on the sidelines. I purposely made friends with the underdogs, those who were forgotten and even teased.

You see, in elementary school I was chubby and on occasion I felt the sting of unkind words. I can't say I was picked on because I found acceptance in my ability to be the class clown, the funny one. By the time junior high rolled around, I decided to skip a lunch and then another and before I knew it, the chubby little girl became thin and acceptance came easy. I had now become an official member of the popular crowd. But that chubby little girl never forgot what it felt like to be overlooked or looked through. I took notice of those left behind and always wanted to help.

By this time, art and the desire to pursue it had all but faded and my pursuit of beauty and creativity would be found in sculpting my body and my social life. Funny, but not funny; rather, sadly true. Though my art teacher did everything in his power to encourage me to attend an art school and further pursue my giftings, I chose the safer route, again to color within the lines. Diet and nutrition would be my choice of careers. Besides, this made much more practical sense, right? In my mind, it was always about what I should do. After all, one must always make the wise decision, avoid risk, and check one's list.

So, off to college I went to become a dietitian. After three years of statistics and chemistry, it was all I had not to lose my creative MIND. After much soul-searching and divine prompting, I ended up in beauty school. Say what? I know, right? But wow, was it a fit! I immediately knew I was built for it, and again, it came easy to me. It was the perfect combination of using my artistic and social skills. I honestly loved every minute of it. Day after day, I helped women feel amazing and beautiful, and I made a friend every half an hour to an hour. What a great gig.

As time went on, my creativity bubbled up in different areas. After getting married and buying our first house, my focus quickly became making that house an inviting home. It became my own personal art project. I lavished my attention on every

PART 1

detail by choosing the perfect colors and gathering random pieces of worn or hand-me-down furniture and accessories. With a little imagination and a whole lot of paint, I made magic! My budget was non-existent, but my creative mind was in overdrive. My dormant art abilities were once again firing on all cylinders and my love for interior design was born. Years went by and all my friends and family called on my untrained expertise in helping them create a beautiful space out of basically nothing.

After twenty-some years of styling hair, I made a difficult decision to retire from a career I loved and travel with my previous husband doing full time ministry. During this time, I took a two-year online course for interior design. I dabbled in design but put it on the shelf to do the more practical thing and take on all the busy, behind-the-scenes work for the ministry. All of this drained and depleted me, much like my three-year college experience. Again, I thought it was the sacrifice a good girl and wife should make and I proceeded without complaint, only to find myself years later in a place I never thought would be my reality because remember, I checked my list not once, but twice!

After 25 years of marriage, I was faced with a situation that flipped my "good girl, good life" rule upside down. The husband I'd known for over 30 years made the decision to no longer follow the rule book and violate the sacred vows we'd taken so many years before. Our marriage reduced to nothing but memories, our life together was now over.

BLINDSIDED, would be the word. As I stood there among the rubble of our divorce, I had no grid for such a reconstruction job. I thought it was such a well-crafted life. Now it looked as if that structure had no redeemable quality; even the foundation was cracked. Was this life of mine salvageable? Was it even worth rebuilding? Quickly, I knew the answer as I looked into the innocent eyes of my young son.

We would need to rebuild, but where should we start?

So, I called on the only one who had the skill, ability, and creativity to see past my current surroundings. **I knew the Great**

Designer would have a plan, and He did! He had the blueprints all along even though He only shares bits and pieces as the building process unfolds. He has been great at sending the right workers at exactly the right time to help reconstruct my life, my heart, and my destiny. Which brings me to my co-authors.

Angela was strategically sent to me years ago in the early stages of my rebuilding. We have walked through much of the rubble together, sifting through the brokenness, hurts, fears, and all the trash left behind by such destruction. The Great Designer sent me the best of the best and she has not only helped me with trash removal; she has helped me shore up my foundation.

Niccie was recently sent to help with my design. She and I are currently working on all the details. We are placing each unique piece I have in its perfect spot. In fact, when people see this redesign, they often say, "I've never seen anything quite like it. I see you've rebuilt and it's so much bigger and better than before. It actually has that WOW factor that everyone desires. Can I ask you who your **designer** is?"

And of course, we gladly give out His name!

Niccie is outstanding at directing people His way. She's so patient as she helps people find the treasures they have packed away. Her organizational skills are out of this world, I might add. When she is done with your design, you'll know where everything's at and how best to use it.

Honestly, this experience has been difficult and even painful at times. It has been a lot of work, I'm not going to lie, but the Great Designer has done such a remarkable job on my makeover that I have decided to also be one of His helpers. I work with Angela and Niccie on one-of-a-kind, incredible makeovers for women seeking their purpose and destiny.

God often speaks to us through parables. For example, in New Testament times, many people were fishermen and they knew their craft inside and out. So, when Jesus wanted to teach them a deep truth, He would speak to them in their unique giftings so they could fully grasp and apply it to their lives. How personal is our God? He is AMAZING! He has been speaking to me in a way I can personally relate to, using the design process.

I now have my own interior design company, Restoration Details, where I help others create beauty in their surroundings, alongside my life coaching business, Life by Design, creating God-given beauty within their hearts. You see, I was built for this by the Great Designer. He used every desire, all my gifts, and all my broken pieces to create the life I now live.

What are you being built for, my beautiful friend?

I have found most women love beauty, design, and transformations. Guess what? So does He! So, in my section of the book, I want to help you uncover and deeply understand His unique and beautiful design for your life—the reason you were BUILT. I am here to help you by **lighting up the present.**

I will be taking you through the renovation of your heart in a fun and easy way you will understand. You will learn how to design the life of your dreams in exquisite detail as you create an inner place of beauty, worthy to house the presence of the Great Designer, the King of Kings!

Meet Niccie Kliegl, Author of Part Three, Blazing into the Future

I hope you are beginning to see how we plan to inspire you into God's great glory. Angela will be helping you stand upon the foundation of truth and light, allowing you to put away the past and ignite a burning fire for what is to come. Barb will open your eyes to the beauty that awaits the royal children of God, lighting up His unique design for your life.

I will help you step into your calling so you can blaze confidently into the future, with rich blessings for you and the Kingdom of our Lord and Savior Jesus Christ.

"Therefore, my brothers and sisters, make every effort to confirm your calling and election. For if you do these things, you will never stumble, and you will receive a rich welcome into the eternal kingdom of our Lord and Savior Jesus Christ" (2 Peter 1:10–11).

Today, I lead an amazing group of sisters and brothers all desiring to live out the call God has on their lives. But don't let this leave you questioning your call. I'm finding very few of us know how we are being called and fewer yet know how to step in fully. This was me, four short years ago. Once I learned how to hear God, *Tap into the Trinity©*, and step in fully, I became unstoppable at helping others to live, love, learn, and lead according to the call God has on their life.

But, like I said, it wasn't always this way.

I was raised in the church and knew God. I loved Him but didn't know how to live into Him, or what that even meant. I knew the Holy Spirit and looking back, I can see we were pretty tight. I learned to listen to Him, but sadly, I wrote Him off, accrediting His promptings to intuition and worldly wisdom.

I knew Jesus died for my sins and I would repent and try to be "good" but more so out of discipline and to avoid condemnation than out of conviction coming from a sweet desire to please Him who gave so much to me.

Do you know what I mean?

I can remember having the most tender heart for the forgotten and downtrodden. People told me I was kind and compassionate. Without knowing God intimately, I adopted an inner confidence when leading and caring for others. This worldly success actually pulled me away from God and His great calling. While being fiercely independent sounds good, it often robs the world of the amazing work He has in store for each of us.

I had learned how to live in the world and was doing it pretty well. I was kind and conscientious and yes, I knew how to love. I thought that was enough. I was happy, making great money, had a sweet little family, and was comfortably settled into what many would call a charmed life. But, thank the Lord, God was not content with me living a half-lived life.

That's what so many of us do, especially those who have lived a fairly unscathed life. We live our idealistic, charmed lives without even knowing the abundance, joy, energy, power, and glory that await us as we learn to turn away from this world—which we believe is serving us well—and rather step into the Spirit and all of His glory.

Sometimes my clients battle feeling worthy of having more when they already have so much or when they've possibly been through way too much. If this is how you feel, I simply want to remind you that you have been handcrafted by the Craftsman of all (Psalm 139). You are chosen and royal (1 Peter 2:9). You have gifts and talents woven into you with free will to use them in a plan that is already predestined for greatness (Jeremiah 29:11, Ephesians 2:10). This greatness isn't only for you. God wants you on His team and as you do His work well, you will be blessed (see Matthew 25:14–30, the story of the talents).

When I was 46 years old, my last child left for college and I was heading into my 25th year of nursing. I'd been a director of nursing most of my career and loved watching my staff grow, my patients heal, and their families find peace. It felt great to do good work.

So why then, out of the blue, was I bored doing the work I once loved? It was because God decided it was **time** to take matters into His own hands. The way I see it, this fire—to lead others into their call—had been burning in me for some time. He had been preparing me during my years as a nursing leader. He took hardships from my past—like my reading disorder and my parents' divorce when I was young—and turned them into blessings for the future.

He wants to do this for you too, for all of us.

So why did He choose to stoke my fire and open my eyes to new light? And why am I now blazing into the future to help others do the same?

The answer has to do with one sweet word and three sweet letters:

A

S

K

After a few months of trying to force passion back into the work I'd once loved, I turned to God for answers. FOR THE FIRST TIME IN MY LIFE, I SOUGHT GOD.

Oh, don't get me wrong. I knew enough of God's power to drop to my knees in times of great fear, but that kind of seeking is short lived. That's seeking out of desperation rather than desire. Using God this way is short lived because when the desperation passes, so does our need for God. **Desiring to know, hear, love, and follow God in your everyday life is powerful beyond belief, and many never tap into it.**

Think about that.

Have you been seeking God fervently with no other reason than a desire to know HIM, hear HIM, and to live into HIM?

This is where you will find your calling.

He is waiting for you and we are here to help stoke that fire, to enlighten this beautiful way of living, and to help you blaze into your God-partnered future.

God has great plans for you and for HIS kingdom!

So, how are we going to get you stepping into your call? I am going to share with you the very steps I used, and still use today with all of my coaching clients.

We are going to get God-partnered like never before. We are going to *Tap into the Trinity*© for a life that far exceeds anything here on earth.

So, find a comfy spot, get out a pen and journal, or scribble all over this book if that is who you are. In my part of the book, you will learn how to apply the ***30-Day Calling Activation Plan*** with a ***3-Step Activation Technique*** for you to truly master the art of ASK—Asking, Seeking, and Knocking your way into God's glory.

CHAPTER TWO

LAND

MY LAND IS IN NEED OF A FATHER, MY REALTOR

I have deeply discovered that exactly as a house needs a healthy structure and foundation to withstand the storms and turbulence of life, so we need a firm foundation from the moment we are born. I often wonder where the big shift happens?

Every precious one is born with an innate knowledge that they are made for greatness. That is, until they have been polluted by the sinful world. Perhaps it's because that baby came out of the throne room where they spent quality time with the Father right before they were given their marching orders to meet up with their earthly family.

For little girls, I believe the desperate need to be noticed is where heaven meets earth. Her little spirit knows the Father in heaven. He knew her before He knit her together in the secret place within her mother's womb. Unknowingly, this powerful force of truth and true identity within her needs her earthly daddy to come into complete agreement with her heavenly Daddy. In her heart, she knows she needs "Thy kingdom to come and Thy will to be done on earth as it is in heaven."

She has a deep desperation here on earth to feel the same affirmation she once knew while sitting on the Lord's lap. We often see this deep longing play out when a little girl starts playing dress up.

"Curl my hair Daddy!"

"Can you buy me a crown Daddy?"

"Do I look beautiful?"

She twirls around in her dress to bring attention to herself.

"Do you see me Daddy?"

"Am I pretty?"

"Am I enough Daddy?"

"Am I captivating?"

She'll grab him by the face and look him dead in the eyes.

"Am I your princess Daddy?"

"Do you see me?"

"Do I have your attention Daddy?"

You will often see her crawling up on her daddy's lap, grab his big hands and wrap his arms around her as if to say, "I need protection Daddy."

"I need to know that you have me covered."

"I feel unsafe and need you at this moment Daddy."

Can you see yourself here? Can you feel those needs? Do you have memories of doing this, or maybe in your heart you longed for this?

A daddy, if harnessed correctly by the heavenly Father's love, is able to bring heaven to earth as he partners with what God did for his little girl before she was brought here. A father is able to provide the platform for that little girl to grow strong, confident, and hopelessly in love with the Savior. Why? Because she then knows the liquid love of God through an earthly man. A great reminder of where she came from. A

PART 1

wonderful affirmation of what she always knew plays out in a fleshly and tangible way.

I would imagine if a little girl spent her most influential and formative years living in the earthly example that parallels the heavenly blueprint, she would grow up vibrating a frequency of heaven that reverberates the heavenly Father's pleasure upon everything she touches. Wouldn't you agree?

A little girl's need for validation and affirmation from her earthly father is not that of a trickle of water but rather of a raging sea.

Although I can't relate as much to the little boy, I speculate that I could figure him out too. Every little boy needs to see the strength playing out in front of him. It's a strength that reflects the perfect Father's Godly example that was imprinted on his little spirit before he was brought here to earth. He needs to see a daddy who looks as bold as a lion but can also be as gentle as a lamb. It's heartbreaking to see a little boy grow up without that healthy example.

Every little boy needs to see a daddy fully engaged with him, a daddy who is able to affirm him and validate his masculinity. That little boy will longingly watch the strength of his father and will ask himself the hard questions that also impact his heart:

"Do I have what it takes Daddy?"

"Will I be big like you someday?"

You will see that little boy dress up in superhero outfits and he'll flex his muscles.

"Am I a man Daddy?"

"Am I big and strong?"

"Am I brave and fearless like you Daddy?"

Yet he is also safe enough with his daddy to be able to show some vulnerability as well.

"Can I love well Daddy?"

"Will I be able to love a lady right?"

"Can I show strength by showing tenderness Daddy?"

A little boy desperately needs his daddy to walk alongside him—not only with everyday manly lessons such as changing a tire, building projects, changing the oil, or using tools; he also desperately needs to see his daddy love a woman well, manage his home with love and honor rather than in anger and with an iron fist. He needs to see his daddy harnessed under the authority of the Holy Spirit, stable yet transparent, strong yet not afraid to admit his faults, confident yet full of humility, hard-working yet not consumed.

I would think if a little boy grew up experiencing the earthly example of a father that parallels the heavenly blueprint, he would also grow up vibrating a frequency. This would be the frequency of heaven that reverberates the heavenly Father's pleasure upon everything he touches as well.

A little boy's need of validation and affirmation from his earthly father is not that of a light tap on a nail head with the hand, but like the force of a sledgehammer smashing down on steel.

What would the world look like if every child grew up understanding the true fruits of the Spirit in a father: kindness, goodness, patience, love, faithfulness, joy, peace, gentleness, and self-control? What if these beautiful qualities were active in daily operation within the home? Would it change the dynamics of personal development, integrity, character, values, and morals? Would it cause them to walk in faithfulness, commitment, loyalty, discernment, and honor? Would it create a domino effect where children would go on to develop healthy homes of their own? Would we see those gifts continue on through our grandchildren and their children?

Now, before we go any further, let me say that grace covers a multitude of inadequacies and sin. This could go one of five ways:

1. You could be the one that reads this and your heart identifies with the deep canyons that were never filled.

2. You might be the one who is in the process of child-rearing right now and feeling frustrated with daily life regrets, feeling that you could do better in raising your children.
3. You may be the one who feels you have a pretty good grip on raising your kids, yet know that you are very much in a process and need to learn more.
4. You may be the one who raised your children already and is watching your adult children's lives fall apart before your very eyes, and wondering where you went wrong. You live with guilt, shame, blame, and condemnation that you didn't do better while they were growing up.
5. You may be the parent who lives in fear of doing the wrong thing, so you are battling daily with control and perfectionism which you see dominating your life and your children's lives every day. Maybe it's hard for them to simply be kids because they are trying so hard to meet your expectations of perfection that they were never meant to fulfill.

We know our earthly father could only give what he had. He is also a product of how he was raised. My earthly daddy did all he could to raise us well, but he carried some very deep wounds. He had a heart to do what was right and many times he did. But he also struggled most of his life with deep anger and regret.

At five years old, he was the victim of assault in his own home. Back in those days, couples didn't commonly divorce, so families were looked down on if they came from a broken home, even the children. He felt the sting of rejection not only within the four walls of his home, but also when he encountered those in the community.

I won't be going into a lot of detail because that's for another book someday, but I want you to know that when my daddy was in his sixties, he started to take a journey down the roads that had created so much pain in his heart. It was not a journey for the weak and it showed me his grit and determination. He wanted to get better, regardless of his age. He longed to see a rich movement of revival, yet he knew that true revival needed to start in his own heart first.

In his silver years, my daddy became a gentle giant in my eyes. We hardly knew him anymore. Jesus radically restored his heart and when he died, I found myself grieving the years during which I hadn't known his gentle side. And I grieved for the years that I had known his gentle side and wished I could have known that side of him for longer.

Had I known the restored side of daddy growing up, I know I would have made life choices out of abundance rather than scarcity. I'm so thankful I was able to witness a transformation of a man whom I loved deeply, right before my very eyes. My daddy . . . my hero.

Sometimes, when we do not have the Godly example of an earthly father, God will send a mentor to pick us up, retrain us, and guide us, so we can rebuild and make something of our lives. "God with skin on," I call it. Are they still out there?

Maybe you've not been gifted with a Godly example of a father or mother, but you can ask for one in your daily prayers. If you don't have that gift yet, you can ask God to heal those places in you so that He is able to breathe new life into your lungs, remind you of the plans and purposes for your life, and set your feet on solid ground.

Fortunately, I was blessed enough to have been gifted a mentor who was not only able to give me what my daddy couldn't, but he was also able to mentor my dad before he died. I want to openly express a thank you to my spiritual father, Urie Hershberger. You helped me to rebuild my foundations and because you partnered with God, I am able to possess my land. You taught me through your love and commitment to go to my true heavenly father for all my resources.

My prayer is that by the time you finish this section, you'll be able to identify every identity issue that enslaves you, no matter what it is. You will be able to locate why you've not been able to possess your land and maintain it well. And you will be able to forgive your earthly daddy, locate where the cracks started on your soil and your land, identify the lies and voids, and get them filled once and for all, so that you will have more equity and be able to give out from that abundance.

Welcome to ground zero. Together we can purchase some land. May the Lord richly bless you and show Himself faithful, committed and present, so that your life will be flowing in its fullest potential. My plan is to show you there is no such thing as going backwards in the kingdom of God. So, if you are feeling like a big failure already . . . DON'T GO THERE!

God always completes what He has started. He is a master investor and He intends on cashing in 100% on the investments He has made in your life. Let's take a look at some of those investments before you were ever created in your mother's womb. God doesn't forget about these deposits and He doesn't want you to forget either.

Let's go backwards to refresh our minds so that we can now go forward.

"Before I formed you in the womb I knew you, before you were born I set you apart; I appointed you as a prophet to the nations" (Jeremiah 1:5).

"You have searched me, LORD, and you know me. You know when I sit and when I rise; you perceive my thoughts from afar. You discern my going out and my lying down; you are familiar with all my ways. Before a word is on my tongue you, LORD, know it completely. You hem me in behind and before, and you lay your hand upon me. Such knowledge is too wonderful for me, too lofty for me to attain. Where can I go from your Spirit? Where can I flee from your presence? If I go up to the heavens, you are there; if I make my bed in the depths, you are there. If I rise on the wings of the dawn, if I settle on the far side of the sea, even there your hand will guide me, your right hand will hold me fast. If I say, 'Surely the darkness will hide me and the light become night around me,' even the darkness will not be dark to you; the night will shine like the day, for darkness is as light to you. For you created my inmost being; you knit me together in my mother's womb. I praise you because I am fearfully and wonderfully made; your works are wonderful, I know that full well. My frame was not hidden from you when I was made in the secret place, when I was woven together in the depths of the earth. Your eyes saw my unformed body; all the days ordained for me were written in your book before one of them came to be. How precious to me are your thoughts, God! How vast is the sum of them! Were I to count them, they would outnumber the grains of sand—when I awake, I am still with you. If only you, God, would slay the wicked! Away from me, you who are bloodthirsty! They speak of you with evil intent; your adversaries misuse your name. Do I not hate those who hate you, LORD, and abhor those who are in rebellion against you? I have nothing but hatred for them; I count them my enemies. Search me, God, and know my heart; test me and know my anxious thoughts. See if there is any offensive way in me, and lead me in the way everlasting" (Psalm 139).

Ground Zero. It's time to invest in some land.

I'm about to tell you a story and so that you don't get lost in the process, I'll give you a hint: the realtor represents my mentor, Urie. And the brokenness I present was the spiritual condition of my life when I met him and his precious wife, Amanda, who is one of my dearest friends. I will forever be grateful that they invested so much into my life.

My appointment went as expected with the realtor. I found myself questioning everything he said. He's a man! Ugh. I haven't been able to trust the men in my life up until now, so this really stretches me to trust him. It had taken me several days to work up the courage to call him. He had left some messages for me on my voicemail but I simply didn't know if I could trust him.

How in the world am I expected to make an investment in my land if I feel like I don't belong anywhere? My entire life I have felt like an orphan or a stranger in a foreign country. I have been misunderstood greatly, betrayed in the deepest ways, and I know the pain of loss far too well. It's so scary to think

PART 1

of settling in one place because this means I will have to put my roots down.

Everyone knows that investing in land is painful. It takes sweat, determination, and hard work. It seems it would be easier to buy a tiny house on wheels so that when someone hurts me, I can move. But I know that God is asking me to plant my feet and settle.

Do I have what it takes? What if those around me judge me for not maintaining my property well? What if they talk about me? Or worse yet, what if they want to be friends? (Gulp). What if I'm not enough for them?

All of my life I've been a performer. I've been able to keep my mask on and hide behind it. I've always loved the theater and plays and I've lived my life as an actress. I can put on a good show that things are good and as they should be. So far, I feel I've been able to fool people pretty well. I am, however, pretty satisfied with myself that I'm finally taking the time to invest in me and my land. My realtor is meeting me several times this week to tour some properties. I hope that I can trust him completely.

The second time I met my realtor I told him I wanted to live near train tracks and he laughed.

"Why?" he asked. "Why would you want noise?"

I told him noise helps to drown out what goes on inside of my head. The noise takes my mind off of myself and helps silence my doubts and insecurities. I learned from an early age how to find things to help me drown out the sounds of fighting, yelling, and crying. Yes, distractions are good because then I don't have to feel anything. I hate feeling. Bring on the train tracks!

My realtor looked at me with kindness and asked, "Well, how has that worked out for you?"

I ignored his question and went on to the next request. "I need lots of trees."

My realtor smiled. "Okay."

Moving right along. "And I want high fences."

My realtor leaned back and put his hand to his mouth as if in deep thought. "And can I ask why?"

My reply was confident and candid. "I like things set in place so others are blocked from seeing me completely."

My realtor met my answer with a smile and a small nod, "I see."

Wow, that was uncomfortable. It was almost like he was reading my mind by the way he looked at me. Wriggling in my seat, I came up with the next statement. His kindness made me blurt things out that I'd never shared with a single soul. "I need my land to be perfect because I can't afford setbacks. Setbacks totally send me into a whirlwind. I like everything perfectly aligned because if unexpected issues arise then I don't feel so . . . well . . . perfect." Gulp. In my head, I was thinking, "I can't believe I just said that."

He smiled. He has the kindest eyes. We talked for quite a while. I found myself being lost in his gaze. They say the eyes are the windows to the soul. It was such a strange feeling. It was as if I had met him before, maybe in my life before I came to earth. Ha, ha! Stop. I'm feeling soft. Ahhhhh, keep it together. The investment would be good. I suppose there may be a higher price to pay later if I don't come under his leadership and guidance now. I want my land to be blessed. I want to raise a family there and if I make this investment now, it will bless them in their future.

After a few ventures I started to trust my realtor more and more. At first, I wanted him to give me the directions and addresses of where I should go, rather than him guiding me. That felt safer to me. But yet I longed for him to guide me. It was the most painful yet wonderful experience of my life.

But what if he would ask me questions about my life, my pain, and my heartache? I simply can't go there. What if I say too much? What if I get uncomfortable? What if he sees through my indecisiveness and confusion while I'm walking through this uncharted territory? I can't take those chances. What if we go to see my land and I lose my footprints, everything

PART 1

I've ever known, and the only set of footprints I have to follow back to safety is his?

Regardless of all my questions, he drew me in to trust him and we were able to locate my dwelling place. It needs a lot of work but I'm hopeful, I think. I can see how overgrown it is. It's filled with a lifetime of unwanted briars, thorns, weeds, chaos, confusion, and control. You can see where wild animals have made their homes within the trees and unwanted intruders have torn up the grounds. Jeez, it kind of feels like my heart.

It's going to take a long time for it to look good again. My realtor warned me that it's a journey not for the faint of heart to fix this property. But he assured me he would never leave me and that he would walk alongside me. He often encouraged me in saying that he saw himself in me. And he said I had the grit and determination to make things work.

Whatever! He doesn't know me. But I have to admit that when he said those words, something inside of me leaped. Could it be true? It really does feel good to have someone believe in me even when I don't believe in myself.

After a week, I was so glad I'd gone with my gut instinct and decided to give my realtor a chance. Friends had told me he was trustworthy but never in my wildest dreams did I imagine he would work as hard as he has.

In a short time, he helped me to understand I was worthy of making my dwelling beautiful. He taught me I was equipped to make a precious space for myself. He also stayed, and he and his wife helped me work every day in cleaning up what didn't line up for my life. Their eyes ooze kindness and love. They show their approval of me and they seem to care about my desires, dreams, and aspirations. Why do they believe in me so much? This is foreign.

Every time my realtor points me to another location that needs to be cleaned up, his tenderness and caring heart encourage me to keep going. He and his beautiful wife have become my biggest cheerleaders. He told me after a month that he sees me as family; this is hard to admit but I truly feel it! I hope I don't jinx myself by saying it. I'm used to people walking in and out of my life after broken promises but this does feel different.

My life has been changing day by day ever since I've decided to give him a chance but the way that he gives me a chance . . . it transforms me! I've never had anyone believe in me so much. He has even opened up to me about his own journey of becoming a realtor. He paid a high price to be in this position. It sounds like he learned from the best and he is no stranger to hard work and training. And that's why he's perfect for this job. He's walked the walk and now he leads others the same way so that they can locate their land and steward it well.

Even though it's hard work to clean up my dwelling from a lifetime of turmoil, I find myself excited to meet my realtor on my property each day. I have blisters and my knees are worn out from kneeling so much (in prayer) to remove the unwanted weeds within my heart . . . oops, I mean land. I keep working with his help. It makes it all so much easier.

I trust his judgment for my life. It feels like his wisdom comes from a higher source. He even makes me laugh at myself at times. Wow! That was something I could never do before. I think I took myself too seriously or perhaps I didn't know that I have what it takes. I was so used to putting on a show to make people think I was perfect. Laughing at myself has felt vulnerable yet uplifting.

I merely needed encouragement, someone to tell me it was okay to not be okay. And this transparency and honesty is starting to become a way of life. It feels FREEING. Wow! I thought I could never say that.

It was imperative for me to trust someone to help me along on this confusing and frustrating journey. And I can see why it was important for me to go with someone who has already cut the hard path. I needed a forerunner and God led me to this amazing pioneering realtor.

After a couple months, my realtor friend feels like family too. Oh, how my heart has needed a safe place to land. He's helping me to see that anything worth contending and fighting for is worth the investment in the end.

Oh, sure it's hard work. I go to bed at night in tears because every time we uncover things on my land, we find more issues that need to be dealt with. But I trust my realtor completely and he helps me to see that my resale value is going to be astronomical. Can you imagine what my property will be worth once the foundational hard work is over? I'll be able to share these valuable experiences and investment tools with others.

I've had a thought. What if I could invest in others like my realtor has invested in me? What if I could speak life to those who are lost and have never invested in their own land? What if I could pay it forward? I'm still very much broken, but it's amazing that I'm even thinking this way. I have hope!

There's something about how I feel when I leave my realtor. He speaks purpose into my heart. Oh, sure, there are times I leave feeling beaten and discouraged, but those times are becoming fewer and fewer. I often feel like I can take on the world. What a switch in my stinkin' thinkin', thanks to my realtor.

After four months of hard foundational work, we are ready to start the driveway. It's a daunting and stressful task. Sadly, my realtor is passing me onto another professional. My realtor said he's learned a lot in his own journey with getting the land prepared but this next guy is the actual Waymaker when it comes to the driveway.

I freaked out for a while as I didn't want my realtor friend to leave me but he calls me every day to help me process what's happening on my property. And, I do know I've got to learn to walk on my own sometimes too.

I'm stronger than I used to be, that's for sure. Besides, I know my mentor has to help others find their land and his job isn't done. He's a gift to many and I want others to experience his knowledge and wisdom as well.

Did you have a strong relationship with your father and if not, why?
In addition to your biological father, do you see yourself in need of a mentor? If so, take a moment to pray. Who is the first person who comes to mind?
What lies have you believed about yourself?
How have these lies affected the way you have viewed relationships, the world, and your destiny?
Do you feel confident that you can restore and steward your land/heart well?

CHAPTER THREE
PATH

I'M IN NEED OF A FRIEND, MY WAYMAKER

My realtor provided the way for me to start believing in myself. It was quite an amazing journey. In my heart, I was an orphan. This has nothing to do with my parents because they did the very best that they could. The orphan mentality had to do with the many injustices I lived through.

My orphan heart affected me in two ways. It pulled me back from engaging in relationships with others, and it pushed people away so they would want nothing to do with me. It worked like that for many years until I realized I'm made for connection. The message was often engraved on my heart, "You're not good enough." "No one cares to hear your heart." "There's something wrong with you because you don't have it all together." Or, "Your value is based on your good behavior and perfect attitude." Can you relate?

My realtor/mentor gave me permission to be real, raw, and honest without hesitation. My ugly feelings weren't met with looks of disapproval or condemnation but only compassion, mercy, and grace. This provided a platform for me to do the same for others.

At some point in my life, I had shut my heart down so that it wouldn't feel pain anymore. I was numb. I stopped paying attention to my own aches. I ended self-care and personal evaluation. I put others first, which is great in theory but I wasn't healthy. I sacrificed my own wellbeing to appease others. Yet I ended up paying the price in my mental, emotional and physical health. I was a peacekeeper.

It's been said that healed people heal people, and hurt people hurt people. My mentor provided a safe place for me to evaluate my own needs and heart again. He gave me permission to feel. He was "Jesus with skin on."

Jesus understands the pain of defeat. He was betrayed by those closest to Him. He performed miracles, signs, and wonders right before the eyes of the people, yet they accused Him of being the devil. He felt hurt and disappointment deeply, and one can't convince me otherwise. And if He created the emotions, that must mean His ability to feel sadness, hurt, and love must be so much greater.

Friend, no one can tell you what you feel is wrong. What you feel is very real to you and your heart. It's time we stop judging people for how they feel and start meeting them where they are. Validating people's feelings are the first step to helping them come away from the orphan mindset. Validation encourages orphans to take dominion here on earth.

Vulnerability looks very different for different people. Many of us were raised in cultures where weakness and ugly emotions meant failure, shame, condemnation, and a reason for a good spanking. Some church leaders haven't known how to handle our negative emotions. Their answer is to send us to the Word or shame us because, "You are a Christian and shouldn't feel that way." It was scary and fear-driven. We were taught from an early age that you don't talk about your feelings and that you really should simply sweep them under the rug. Where were we to go for a safe place?

I'm convinced the midlife crisis that everyone talks about is nothing more than cellular level trauma, pain, and memory that finally comes to surface because we can't hold it in any longer. Our bodies are like huge memory cards and we hang on to trauma, lies, and woundedness down to the cellular level.

At some point God says, "I love you way too much for you to stay stuck where you are, my child." In His goodness, He will allow the perfect storm so that He can touch you where you have been locked up. He is able to stop in His power what He won't in His wisdom. If He knows it will set you free and draw you near to Him, then He'll allow some things to take place.

If you are never rubbed wrong by various people and their personalities, then how would you ever know your need for Christ? He uses people and messy situations to touch the broken places within us.

For example, a betrayal in a relationship could touch a deeply embedded hurt from childhood where you felt abandoned or left to fight on your own. And God wants to heal the root so you are unmovable and unshakeable.

The question remains: will you and can you be vulnerable with Him? Or will you see Him the way you saw your mean father, controlling mother, insecure grandmother, messed up church leadership, or whoever?

The time may come when you will have to lay yourself down and be real. When I see people stuck in patterns of defeat, I often ask, "How's that working out for you so far?" Chances are if it didn't work out the first forty years of your life, it won't work out during the next forty.

Aren't you tired? Brokenness is hard, healing is hard, but we have to choose our *hard*. My spiritual father taught me how to choose the *hard* that led to redemption and restoration. And that, my friends, is lasting!

I also needed to forgive those who didn't know how to properly care for my heart. Without question, I'm sure they were never given a safe place for their heart either. And so, when I dumped my garbage on them, they didn't know how to handle it because they were never taught. When we aren't raised in a culture of vulnerability, it makes us very uncomfortable when someone is vulnerable with us and expects direction and answers.

Transparency is a tool that God gave us. During the process of a caterpillar becoming a butterfly, right before the cocoon is ready for the big reveal, it becomes transparent and ugly at the same time. Have you ever noticed the beautiful golden ring around the cocoon? My mama pointed that out to me one time. It's almost like that golden ring speaks promise during the pressure. Now we could easily take a knife and slice that cocoon down the center to help that butterfly while it's fighting inside. But if we did that, it would fall to the floor, unable to fly.

You see, the struggle is where the spiritual muscle is built. The integrity of the wings is established and created throughout the pushing and stretching and hard work. In our lives, transparency is something that is needed for us to be real with each other and our God. He is nothing but truth and expects the same from us.

But then the enemy throws a monkey wrench in the plans. I'm sure he has it all set up. He plans to give us pain in relationships so that we guard our hearts. He divides homes so that we build walls. He creates word curses and hate so that we start believing lies. And soon we find ourselves hiding, not willing to bare our hearts. It's simply too painful!

Self-isolation is a tool of the enemy. We were never meant to be alone. We were designed for human interaction and connection. Sure, there are times we need to get away and be alone for a while. Jesus did that. But we aren't meant to stay there. Sooner or later, we have to come out.

Jesus was so transparent when He hung from the cross. I shudder when I think of the vulnerability He showed as He hung there—cold, bruised, naked, and shamed. He looked ugly

PART 1

to the world. It is such a picture of the walk we make on this earth and the wickedness that's done to us. And then He died and into the tomb He went.

We go there on our earthly walk too—into hiding. And unfortunately, that's where the enemy wants to keep us . . . in the tomb of death. And that's where many churches stop. They show us what Christ did on the cross but they don't equip us to go any further.

But what about what happened on the other side of the cross? Resurrection and life were given to Jesus. We have that too!

We are overcomers because of the Overcomer who lives in us. Have you ever wondered why God loves us so much? Because He sent His Son to die for us, and now His Son lives in us. He loves every fiber of us too.

Jesus was the spiritual picture of that cocoon wrapped in the gold lining of God's promises. When He hung, He was transparent. When He broke free, He became the butterfly for all to see.

Have you ever really looked at a butterfly's wings? There's actually no vibrant color on the outside. It's only when the butterfly opens up and reveals itself that we can see its true beauty.

Are you getting what I'm saying here? Transparency is the enemy's biggest fear. When we become transparent, the Lord frees us to become something beautiful. Because we have the light of Jesus on the inside, our colors and freedom shine through for all to see.

My heart's cry is for all of you to be transparent. I long for you to see yourself as that cocoon covered by God's golden thread. I can't wait to see the soaring butterflies you become.

A friend once asked me, "Who do you relate to when you pray? God, Jesus, or the Holy Spirit?" It took me a while to realize my answer was definitely Jesus. I saw Jesus as my friend. It was hard to connect with God as a Heavenly Father because things were not always good with my earthly father. If your earthly father doesn't do a great job reflecting the Heavenly

Father's love then it's hard to trust the Heavenly Father. If our hearts struggle in connecting with our mother, then it's hard to trust the Holy Spirit.

The Holy Spirit was left here for you after Jesus rose from the dead and ascended back to heaven. The Holy Spirit knows you intimately and personally. He watches you as you wake each morning and sees you as you lay your head down on your pillow each night. He knows your ways and your habits. He is your comforter and friend. He knows all of your secrets and disappointments. He is your confidant and nurturer. When we haven't been nurtured by our mother then it's hard to connect with the Holy Spirit. Sadly, the Holy Spirit is often the forgotten one. He stands at the doorway and knocks. "Let me in! I was left here for you when Jesus rose again. I'm here to help! Why have you pushed me away?"

Jesus was my connection to heaven because I had areas I was still hurting to work through with the other parts of the Trinity. My realtor/mentor, Urie, showed me that my dwelling here on earth (Land/Body) was purchased because Jesus paid the price for me. I was no longer an orphan or a foreigner in my land. Once we run to Jesus, the enemy has to go through Him to get to us. Now that's encouraging.

Would you walk with me on this journey? Slip your hand into mine and let's walk together. The hardest journey is not the walk itself. The hardest journey is the twelve inches from your head to your heart. We normally spend half our life living from our head knowledge but now it's time to get your heart to believe what your head has always known. It's an adventure that takes courage, endurance, and tenacity. And as a spiritual mother, I want to say, "You can do it. You have what it takes. Barb, Niccie, and I are with you. Don't give up! Let's go meet Jesus and see how He is able to continue our rebuilding process.

Now, let's build a driveway on our land!

Several weeks went by and Waymaker was very kind. I'm so glad that I listened to my realtor/mentor. This driveway has been hard work to say the least. I was amazed by the foundational

PART 1

preparations that needed to be made in order for my path or driveway to stay straight and narrow. As we began to build the path, from time to time we would see places where the sides would fall away. Typically, this would happen when I would veer too far to the left or to the right. But Waymaker taught me day by day how to drive or walk down the middle so that my path could stay firm and steady.

In talking to Him, I discovered there's a reason I dubbed Him "Waymaker." He truly paid a price for His position. He moved into this area with His young earthly mother and father. I remember Him mentioning their names were Joseph and Mary. He was a baby at the time. He jokes with me all the time about how He was born in a barn amongst the cows and chickens. But I guess His Father is rich as He lives in a mansion made for a King now. I've never seen it but I sure hope that someday He takes me there.

Waymaker learned the trade of carpentry for a good part of His life. He made a lot of beautiful things. He shared stories with me about how He saw people like pieces of wood. They threw themselves away with no intention of making anything beautiful out of themselves. He would climb into the dirtiest and nastiest places to salvage these pieces of wood. He said He could look at them and see their potential through His Father's eyes. It was a gift His Dad gave Him, to be able to see past the rubbish. He would then start whittling away. He would cut off the unsightly pieces and save the good. He would sometimes burn off what wasn't pleasant with fire and at times leave the pieces sitting overnight so they could cool and heal before He would start working again. He called that process "the Refiner's Fire" and through it He made beautiful masterpieces from people who others saw as trash and ruined goods.

His stories captivated me and gave me hope for my future. He would light up when He talked about creating beautiful things. You could see His creative juices flowing but more than that, the love that poured out of His words as He talked about refining His work.

But at times, I would also see sadness. Deep sadness. He shared that He endured great heartache as He taught people along the way about creating a safe path. He endured a lot of conflict as He tried to convince people to believe in the construction of this narrow road.

Haters ridiculed Him and made fun of Him, yet He remained faithful and steadfast in His relationships. This encouraged me so much. He said that He simply kept forgiving them because His Dad taught Him to forgive. He said, "My Father told me to forgive them for they know not what they do."

Wow! I have some people in my life whom I need to forgive and look at through the Waymaker's eyes. Asking for professional help with my path was so wise. I'm so glad my realtor/mentor directed me to Him. My realtor has developed a very special and unique relationship with the Waymaker and he led me to Him. Waymaker talks highly of my realtor. This is one of the best decisions I have ever made.

Due to the Waymaker having specialized in cutting this hard path, He's been able to help me get the job done quickly and efficiently. All I had to do was ask for His help and BAM, He was there and available with big open arms.

I have found there is great reward in following Waymaker. He cut the path on my land, which honestly feels like my heart now because I love it so much. I needed my path to be functional, display eternal value, pleasing to the Waymaker, and long lasting.

I tell you, friends, He poured His blood into this path for me. I watched Him labor in love for my dwelling. There were times He would disappear and I would find Him in the cool of the day among the trees and wildflowers, crying. I often asked Him if He was okay and He would tell me He was a *feeler*. Whatever that is . . .

He said that sometimes when He was around me, He would have to slip away and call His Father and His Helper to pray for me. Can you believe that? He actually cares and intercedes on my behalf! He said He's able to pick up my emotions and

PART 1

motives, my pain and disappointments. I wanted Waymaker to merely cut a path for me but He takes it one step further every day and He carries my burdens as well.

Waymaker never pushes me away when I come looking for Him in the secret place; in fact, He often asks me to sit with Him at His right side. He actually gives me confidence to enter His secret place. I listen to His prayers and they wash me deeply. His cries cleanse my conscience and I come away with a clear mind. I don't know how He does it but somehow, by spending time with Him, I feel justified, reconciled, and redeemed. I don't even have to work for it. He simply does it while I'm with Him. I pray this heart of mine is always open to receive His grace and truth.

Waymaker is able to whisper into my ears and tell me good things I thought I would never hear. When He declares these truths over me, I see His words become alive and active over my life. What He says always comes to pass. It's amazing.

I have truly never met anyone so kind and giving of Himself. He's long suffering. What an honor it is to have Him working on my dwelling.

Waymaker was also careful about selecting the right place for my path. He said there's only one way and that I must be careful and cautious to not veer from the path He cut for me. He laid the foundation and He said it didn't matter whether my house was uphill or down in the valley; He assured me His path would be able to withstand anything heavy or weight-bearing. He also talked to me about making a good drainage system for my path so when the heavy rains came—and He assured me they would—nothing would swallow up or cover up my path to keep me from finding my way. Thank God!

He said the drainage system would be made clear to me. It would consist of connections He would provide—one or two people who would be safe and trustworthy for me to go to when the storms come. They would help me to remove the high waters so my path would not be consumed. He said that at times, those people would even lift my arms for me when I feel too weak on my own.

He explained the victory in my battle. He told me I won't be able to take on my enemies with intellect, reasoning, or sheer willpower but that I need to understand the POWER in who He is as a Waymaker. Those people whom He would send my way in covenant relationship will be able to help me take authority over my enemies and storms. What a big relief to have backup. I've always felt so alone on this journey.

This path was made right! I bet Waymaker's Daddy is so proud of Him. What a sacrifice He has seen His Son make. I am so glad Waymaker is no longer a foreigner in my land. I want Him to know I respect Him greatly and honor Him.

Did I mention that Waymaker also cried when He played in my soil? He poured His sweat and His tears into it. He did! He made sure the soil was stable. He told me how wide, and deep, and long His love was for my dwelling. He explained that the soil was the perfect design and combination to make my path strong. He said it was created like that before the beginning of time. He would often sift the soil through His hands and say, "Do you hear that? Do you hear that sound? This earth groans for you to find your rightful place on this land. There's only one you and this earth needs you to fulfill what's been written in your book of life."

And there were times I would find Him weeping and groaning as He played in the dirt. I would ask Him, "Waymaker, what are you feeling now?" He would lift His tear-stained face, look at me, and say, "I'm just partnering with the groanings I hear from your dwelling, my friend. I'm so excited for you to take dominion here. You are needed here. I have waited for this day. I have waited for you to partner with Me so that we can do great and mighty things together."

Those eyes, WOW, they are as deep as the sea but as beautiful as the heavens. Where have I seen those eyes before? Oh yes, through my realtor. They say birds of a feather flock together. These two—the realtor and the Waymaker—look

PART 1

alike. Maybe as I spend time with Waymaker, my eyes will draw people into love too.

To my surprise, as Waymaker was wrapping up the job on my path, He handed me the bill and you will never guess what it said. He had stamped it with what looked like red ink that said in big, bold letters, "PAID IN FULL." Honest to goodness. I would never lie to you. All of my life, I have never been given something so valuable for free. I have done all I can to save, do right, budget, perform, and make sacrifices. I have done all I can to pay for my own path and yet, in only three days, He laid His life down for me, and took care of the entire price for me. My debt was paid in full!

I called my realtor/mentor in shock to see if maybe I misunderstood, but he laughed and said, "Oh, I forgot to tell you. He does that for everyone who will allow Him onto their land. He's the gift."

I sat there with my mouth hanging open. I thought if I worked hard enough, I would pay for it all, but He literally gave it to me. It suddenly dawned on me that it was never about my own work. He planned to cover it all for me right from the very beginning. Had I known He would give me such a gift, I would have given Him more of my time among the trees and flowers. I would have taken more time to learn from Him. I was so busy working to pay my way that I missed the most important part—Him! All I needed to do was to rest and let Him do His work.

I have tried since then to put together an estimated cost of what price He paid and it honestly brings me to tears. He gave me all of Him! When I think about what He invested into my path, I want to weep. He bled, He cried, He labored, He agonized, He sweat, and He showed up on the job without question, every moment of the day. Why? Because He said I was worth the investment. Wow! Thank you Waymaker.

I pray the day comes when I can partner with Him and see the same value within myself.

Did you ever feel you had to perform or be on good behavior to be validated or noticed?
Were you ever overlooked, abused, or mistreated for having negative emotions? If so, are you able to forgive?
Are you able to be vulnerable and honest with Jesus about your negative emotions? (He already knows what you are thinking. Maybe, He is just waiting for you to be honest.)
Who do you relate to when you pray: Heavenly Father, Jesus, or Holy Spirit?
How does this relationship and connection parallel to your Heavenly Father/earthly dad, Jesus/friendships and siblings, Holy Spirit/mother?
Do you have safe people in your life who can help you process life's storms? Who? (If not, you can start praying for God to send them to you.)

CHAPTER FOUR
GARDEN

I'M IN NEED OF A MOTHER, MY HELPER

A mother's role plays an instrumental part in the development of her little ones. When mentoring women of all ages, I often hear the same cry from the wilderness of their hearts:

"Mom wasn't present."

"Mom didn't protect or stand up for me."

"Mom didn't nurture me."

"Mom was controlling when her life was out of order."

These are only a few of the many examples of mothers' own identity issues which then affect the development of her offspring.

Again, I would like to remind you that your mother and father are also products of their circumstances. They can only give what they had and if their love vaults were never supplied with the right currency, they wouldn't be able to pay out sufficient funds to keep your heart from going into the negatives. As your earthly daddy is supposed to be an example of your Heavenly Father, so your mother is an earthly example of the Holy Spirit—your helper, confidant, nurturer, safe place, and present help in time of need.

Do you struggle with connecting to the Holy Spirit? Maybe you harbor hurts from your mother.

Bank vaults are an interesting word picture when it comes to how a mom unveils the heart of her children and even the heart of her husband. A bank vault is full of wealth. And a mother is gifted with the ability to open the vault for her children, where the wealth is, if she is properly harnessed by the Holy Spirit.

It takes two keys for a mother to operate the vault for her children. The Holy Spirit holds the master key and the mother holds the other key. The two keys require one ridge to be able to access the open door. The Holy Spirit partners with mama in that ridge to unlock the vault of wealth and wisdom for her children. And exactly as if mama works as a bank teller, she must learn to be trusted with the goods that have been given to her. She should have knowledge when the funds are running low and quickened in her spirit when the children need a raise (words of affirmation).

In 2019, I was sitting at my kitchen table and I saw in the spirit two big golden keys laid down in front of me. They were unique keys and somehow, I knew they worked together and one couldn't work without the other. Within a couple of months, a visiting pastor gave me a word he believed was from the Lord. He said God was going to be giving me a set of keys. He said these would not be ordinary keys, but rather master keys. These keys would not only unlock one door they fit; they would be master keys that fit many doors within people's hearts. These keys would unlock universal truths, meaning the foundational truths God would give me would be able to unlock hearts of people no matter what race, ethnicity, or geographical location.

He said, "These will be the keys that unlock a situation where people feel there is no hope."

PART 1

In my spirit, I knew this had something to do with the heart of mothers.

As you grow in the Lord, you will find He is a God of confirmation. He will often provide you with answers from unlikely sources to confirm a word He gave you. This is how you know you are hearing His voice. However, everything should be weighed out with prayer, discernment, and the Word. There is no question that these keys will only be given as I press into the Lord because He is the owner of these keys.

This word is humbling and scary at the same time. It tells me that the Lord trusts me with some treasures, but I know I must maintain a heart of humility to receive any special gifts from the Father. None of this is by my own power or might but only by the price that Jesus paid on the cross for me.

We have to be cautious with these types of visions and given words because it would be very easy to move into pride. We are personally responsible before the Lord, with fear and trembling, that our character is able to sustain the giftings He chooses to give. These giftings do not mean we are better than others. We are all on the same playing field in the kingdom—servants of the Most High God, bought and paid for by the blood of Christ.

I believe wholeheartedly that a mother's connection with her child has an impact that determines whether or not they go on to be world changers. We women give birth in the natural through agony, pain, and transition. Through sweat, tears, transparency, rawness, and humility, we bring life into the world. I believe this gift of earthly birthing is parallel to what we can provide in the spirit.

As I said before, we can unveil the hearts of our children by not allowing pain to stop us. We can help our children push through any circumstance by laying a foundation of transparency and vulnerability ourselves. We can provide a safety net for children to follow suit. We can teach our children how to push through all of life's heartaches and trials and breathe fresh wind into their lungs. Exactly like we birth in the natural, we can birth life in the spiritual by speaking words of affirmation, wholeness, belief, and encouragement into our children's everyday lives.

We are given one of the greatest honors: raising up our children to serve the Lord. Our children are never to fulfill our own purposes, goals, love voids, agendas, or identity. We are never to use them as a way to accomplish what we could never accomplish. We are never to coerce them to live or carry out our dreams and visions.

When we were raised in an unhealthy environment, we often look to our children as a way to redeem our own shattered lives. This is a big NO NO. Our children were never meant to save us or cover our deficits or inadequacies. We are strictly a representation of heaven to push them toward Jesus, to complete His purposes and vision for their lives. They were created for a specific plan and our only job is to make sure they walk into His heavenly blueprint, not our own. Humbling, I know.

The scriptures say, "The tongue has the power of life and death, and those who love it will eat its fruit" (Proverbs 18:21).

When a child is birthed into this world and then abandoned emotionally, that immediately hammers a lie into that child's mind that they were left and forsaken. As they are small and not mature enough to reason through things like we do as adults, the enemy jumps pretty quickly at the chance to whisper in their ears:

"You are all alone."

"There's no one here to fight for you."

"Nobody cares for you."

With those lies embedded in their minds, the enemy has a loophole or open access door to continually pound that same lie and message into their hearts. As they grow into their teenage years and then into adulthood, the lies will be validated over and over and over again, as hurtful experiences happen throughout their lifetime. Once the lies are in place that they are all alone, any circumstance that touches that will seem valid.

Satan is an opportunist and he never plays fair. If he can get a person to believe the lie early on, they will continue to choose relationships and partnerships that only confirm the lie. They will always believe they are not worth fighting for. Brokenness draws brokenness and your child may end up choosing unhealthy relationships with unhealthy people. If the enemy sees an open door to exploit a child in an area left weak by mom and dad, others will come along and try to step into a place of stewardship over that child's heart. You will then find your child in unhealthy boyfriend and girlfriend relationships, and eventually they may choose a marriage partner who either keeps that lie cycle going or feeds the fire.

This is why it's so important for mom and dad to give their children validation. If they know who they are in the Lord, they will have greater respect for themselves, and they will have good morals and values. If they go into a marriage with their love tanks empty from mom and dad, they will look to their spouse to fill that emptiness. That's a very tall order for someone to fill when they are not the one who created the hole to begin with. And it leads to a very unsatisfactory marriage with unfulfilled expectations.

Guard your children's love vaults with all diligence. Defend their hearts, listen well, admit your own faults, and speak protection so they are not left open, vulnerable, and eaten up by other voices. Mama bears should protect the integrity of their cubs' hearts with all due diligence and fervor. As God's love is a consuming fire, we parents can carry a love of consuming fire that leaves nothing untouched in the hearts of our children.

Right now, at this moment, you may be a teenager or an adult who feels bitterness or unforgiveness because you never received the umbrella of protection you so deserved from your mother. Forgiveness is a process. God knows that all too well. You may say that you forgive but still feel that cutting knife when you are around your mother. The enemy may then beat you up with accusations like, "You will never be forgiven because you can't forgive."

Biblically, this is true; however, God created forgiveness and He sees every web of confusion and heartache. He knows the process of what it will take for your heart to really experience true forgiveness. He honors that you are willing to speak of forgiveness and He will meet you there for the rest of the process. So, rest in Him and believe in your heart that you are a good person and want reconciliation. Stop listening to the enemy and allowing him to beat you up because the forgiveness hasn't yet been fulfilled.

I often think of the journey Jesus took to Calvary Hill. He had to carry His heavy cross that would soon be stood upright so that He could die on it. That process of Him carrying the cross had to have been so hard. It was heavy—as your burdens can be heavy. It was awkwardly big—as your hurts can cause discomfort and uneasiness. Moving up the hill with the weight of that cross must have been almost impossible.

But don't forget He was beat, betrayed, abused, and tormented before He was ever expected to carry the weight of that cross. Your journey to forgiveness looks much the same. The weight of what you carry is heavy with the memories of all the painful moments. The Lord understands your walk to Calvary Hill. He knows it's a process. But here's the great news, friend: He is with you and He will see you through so you can come into complete forgiveness.

I always say I was changed when I started to believe in God, but I was transformed when I came to the realization that He believes in me. This is a partnership with the God of the universe. He understands all of your ways and He's committed to you. The processes we have to walk in are exactly why we need His grace and mercy daily. We can't do it on our own.

In ministry, I've heard women cry they feel so guilty because they know the Word says in Ephesians 6:2 that they must honor their father and mother, which is the first commandment with a promise. These broken individuals carry large amounts of guilt because they feel like they are not honoring their parents if they haven't forgiven them completely. I want to extend some words to you that I believe will set you free in this area. I do believe that honor paves the way to restoration; however, respect and honor are difficult to give when they haven't been earned. Forgiveness is a process and the Lord is faithful to carry us through when He knows our heart's desire is to do what's right in His eyes.

In other words, if mom or dad doesn't give respect and honor to you, then it's hard to give it back. Honor also looks different than what the world portrays. Honor is speaking truth when we see our loved ones doing things that don't align with their God-given destiny. Many believe that true honor means keeping our mouths shut when wrong is done, which is not correct. Honor is not about being peacekeepers but rather peacemakers. Peacemakers speak the truth in love and never align with actions that do not carry the character and nature of Christ.

Only the Lord can guide us in our delivery of these hard truths. We never want to correct out of our soul-level where shame, blame, and condemnation can be heard. We want to bring loving correction from a heart of forgiveness with no agenda of our own but simply to see our loved ones walk in their full purpose in Christ Jesus.

Forgiveness doesn't mean that the offenses against you are okay; it means that what Jesus did on the cross was enough to cover them. Do you believe in the power of the cross? Scriptures also state several times that the iniquity of the parents are on the children and can be passed to the third and fourth generations. I truly believe that Jesus died to pay the price for all of these iniquities so that our children and their future children will be blessed. I make this point to show you that honoring your parents can be a lot easier if you take the time to evaluate the relationships they had with your grandparents when they were growing up.

If we can see a pattern of abuse then we are able to extend grace, forgiveness, and honor a lot easier, knowing our dear parents are only giving what they know. Seeing it by the Spirit instead of hating the flesh allows the Holy Spirit to work more thoroughly in recovering the relationships. God is not wringing His hands over this situation. He's not pacing the floor wondering what in the world He's going to do with you and your parents. He has seen it all. He saw every offense that led to the dominoes falling down in your blood line, and He's not taken off guard by it. He's all-knowing and you can trust Him.

Now, it's time to work in my gardens and flowerbeds. Are you ready?

Waymaker told me He would send His Helper over today. Evidentially, this is a normal part of the Triune co-op. I had yet to meet the Big Guy of the organization but by now I trusted the process and I couldn't wait to meet Helper. I wondered right away if His eyes would glisten and draw me in like the others.

Day after day went by and Helper never came. I finally reached out to Waymaker to see if He knew how I could contact His Helper. He said the most shocking thing.

He said, "Oh, Helper has been there all along. I left Helper there for you."

I answered, "What? Where?"

I decided to take a walk and survey my dwelling to find Helper. I assumed I would find Him in the woods among the trees and wildflowers where Waymaker used to go to get away, but no one was there. It was a wild experience. Even though I couldn't see Him, it was almost like I could feel the presence nearby.

After hours of searching, I cried out, "Okay Helper, I know you are here. I don't see you but I sense you. I'm asking you to show yourself to me. Would you come and make yourself known to me?"

Suddenly, I was filled! To this day, I cannot explain what happened but I sensed I was being encouraged, nurtured, and empowered all at once. It was a supernatural encounter of goodness and love all wrapped up in one. A love I've never felt in my entire life.

I'm not sure if I mentioned this before but there was a house already on my dwelling and by walking around, I could clearly see the outlines of all the old landscaping and gardens.

PART 1

At some point, I'm sure they were beautiful but I was now left with a meager and scraggly mess. It made me exhausted even to think of the hours and tears I would have to invest into this part of my dwelling.

Helper encouraged my heart and led me first to the gangly fruit trees. You could see it had been an entire lifetime since the branches had been pruned or cut back. I walked to the old shed to pull out the wooden ladder and shears. Regret gripped my heart at the thought of chopping away at these innocent trees. They appeared to be beautiful and strong standing but they hadn't produced a good yield of fruit for years.

I climbed up to the top of the ladder and started sending limb after limb of diseased and unhealthy wood to the ground below. I hadn't noticed along the way how sad and lopsided these trees were looking until I had finished and took a step back to really look. I felt Helper lean in and come near as my heart felt sadness and disappointment.

"Why did I cut so much off, Helper? I've made them look so hideous."

Helper gently spoke into my ear and said, "I know it hurts when we cut the dead off and prune what's not useful, but I promise you that if you trust me in this process, I'll help you grow good fruit."

Suddenly I realized that if these trees had been raised up in the way they should go, they probably wouldn't have needed so much self-care now. There was no question in my mind that in order for me to produce the kind of harvest Helper wanted me to produce, I would have to cut away what wasn't good.

"Oh, but it hurts!" I cried out.

"I know," Helper answered. "But I'm never going to leave you. Trust me my child; when you make it through this hard season, you will thank me. Spring is on the way."

There were times I felt regret for inviting Helper into my pruning process but I knew that just like any other relationship, I was going to have to learn how to listen and press in so that my heart would know how to respond in love.

Helper seemed to give me more strength as the days went on and I learned to trust in the process. How could I expect to see change overnight when I was working with a lifetime of my dwelling left ignored, unattended, and without training? With Helper's encouragement in my spirit, I started dragging each piece of diseased wood, scalped branches, and useless twigs over into what I would call a compost pile. Little did I know at the time how big this pile of unsightly refuse would actually grow to be.

Next, I decided to start cleaning up the flowerbeds. I thought, "Where do I even start?" I felt overwhelmed by the weight of what my eyes were taking in. I'm sure that at one time, these beds displayed greatness and wafted fragrance of beauty and unity but they certainly didn't now.

Helper felt my defeat and nudged my heart. "You know, when you allow seeds of discord and unhealthy roots, they produce runners and shoots. If left unattended, they take over every area of your dwelling."

My heart sank. How did it get so far out of hand? I rolled up my sleeves and decided to partner with Helper in digging up every root that wasn't pleasing for my dwelling. I was astounded by the truth of what Helper spoke. It was absolutely amazing to see how the bad roots produced root systems so deep and so wide. If there had been anything beautiful planted there, it would have been swallowed up by the unwanted roots.

When all was finished, I added those discards to my compost pile. I stood in shock as I looked upon that heap of scraps in front of me. Helper knew my thoughts and said, "Don't be discouraged. That pile of garbage may look unsightly now, but trust me when I tell you whatever is thrown there will be used later. I would never ask you to throw something away if I knew we couldn't use it for greater purposes down the road."

Peace came in and I knew in my heart I was called according to this purpose and that all things would work together for my good.

PART 1

This process took a few weeks. Helper was gentle yet firm in the directions that were given. We partnered together so well. I looked forward to meeting Helper in the gardens each morning and laying under the trees together each afternoon. Yes, Helper chose the same exact spot to rest in as Waymaker—among the trees and wildflowers. They are so much alike.

One afternoon, I took a nap in the shade to rest my aching bones, and I woke up to find Helper waiting with great anticipation to show me something. I picked myself up off the ground, straightened my straw hat, and proceeded out of the woods, carefully following Helper's footsteps. I began to trust Helper's nudges on my heart and I had trusted the guidance enough by now to know this next lesson must be really good.

Helper took me to the corner of my dwelling, down in a small valley, and showed me a patch of beautiful flowers I had never noticed before. Well, maybe I had noticed them at one time but because I was so discouraged by my dwelling's disruptions, I had put them aside and chose not to look there again. Oh, did those flowers and plants ever look sad. At one time, I'm sure those little flowers brought great appreciation and promise but they now appeared to be dying because they had been forgotten.

Helper watched me survey the condition of the tender petals and said, "I brought you down into this valley of unfulfilled vision because I wanted to see if you ever thought these flowers could live again. The truth is, they've always been here but because of your distractions, you forgot to nurture what was still good and lovely."

Then Helper placed His hand over my heart and I felt warmth, love, and power rise up within. Helper then told me to prophesy life over the dry places in that little flower bed and when I did, I began to see the flowers start moving and life came into them. I could sense Helper's approval for my actions and then I heard, "Do you have places where promises have died, dreams have been squashed, and visions have gone away? Do you have places in your families, friendships, or other areas that are giving you death instead of life? It's time to sing my Word over them and then watch an army rise from your circumstances, Child. You were made for more! And I want to raise up your dry places and disappointments through your prophetic worship to me."

My legs started to shake and I fell down on my knees in tears. Had I given up hope? Only Helper would have known that. I'm so thankful for my new friend.

Helper was kind and caring and didn't give me more than I could handle. I was directed to take a few days and rest so that my mind and heart could heal from all the work that had been done in such a short time. I found if I didn't fight the process but rather leaned into the Helper, the process went a lot quicker. My submission to Helper's leadership and authority was scary at first but as I allowed Helper to carry me through, things didn't drag on. Rest seemed to be a weapon of my warfare. Rest was hard for me when I came from such a work mentality. Helper taught me the treasure and value of rest.

After those days of deep rest and rejuvenation, I woke up excited, anticipating to what Helper would be introducing me next. I was beginning to love the journey because I was seeing the beautiful fruit of my labor. It also really helped that I now knew I couldn't walk alone. Helper mentioned I would be introduced to the Big Guy of the Triune co-op, yet I sensed I still had one more lesson on my dwelling. I was raring and ready to go, like a kid in a candy store. I love doing life with my Helper.

My heart was directed by that nudge I've grown to love with everything within me, and I was led to the edge of my property. I was facing a very big and terrifying eyesore that was clearly neglected. My dwelling is surrounded by a hedge of protection that Waymaker told me would be there once I accepted Him into my space. I could see where an enemy or critter had tried to break through that hedge of protection. Actually, I was looking at a gaping hole and I didn't feel so safe anymore.

PART 1

Helper bent over and began to cry with groanings so deep I was sure those cries were being ripped from the deepest core. I stood quiet and hot tears started to stream down my cheeks. I raised my hands and asked Waymaker and Helper how I could partner with them so I could be released from this heavy burden. My stomach actually hurt from the pain of what was being released from the depths of my heart. My cries felt good, they felt right, and it was clearly time for me to feel the pain and release it once and for all.

Suddenly, I heard Helper stop wailing and I sensed a hand in front of my face. A bottle was there, held by the firm hand of Helper, to collect all of my tears. My cries diminished to a sniffle and I looked up again to see where Helper went.

Helper was dumping those tears on my compost pile. I couldn't believe my eyes. But why? My questions were quickly met with Helper's words of gentle kindness and goodness. "I keep track of all your sorrows. I collect all of your tears in my bottle. I record each one in my book and your tears of release will be what waters the fertilizer for your tomorrow."

Then Helper turned back to that hole in my wall and firmly stated, "You were never meant to build your own walls of protection. You have an enemy and little critters that hate your gardens. They find open doors and crevices to slip through, where you have not trusted my guidance and protection. They sense fear and they will try to take over and eat all of your fruit if they detect you aren't strong enough to come against them. This is where you need to remember the Blood that Waymaker shed for you. This is not your battle to fight alone. When you plead the Blood of Waymaker, you are declaring your position and belief in Waymaker to the enemies of your soul and dwelling. Day by day, I want you to pray for a revelation of the power of the Blood because it is so vital for you to walk in victory. When the accuser attacks you, the Blood is your defense and authorizes you to push back the darkness that's trying to invade your dwelling. Do you understand me?"

I shook at the reality of the Helper's words and everything in me connected with the power that was spoken. The Blood of my Waymaker speaks of better things and I will never need to fight alone.

Helper paused to give me time to process, and then with pure love spoke one last thing that I'll never forget as long as I live. "Remember this, child—Waymaker's real name is Jesus!"

PART 1

Do you struggle in your relationship with the Holy Spirit?

Was your mother able to meet your heart's needs? Was she able to bring out the best in you?

Do you believe that what Jesus did on the cross is enough to cover your sins or those sins done against you?

Do you sense that the Helper, Holy Spirit, wants to do a pruning in the garden of your heart?

Do you believe that God can use your discards, discouragements, and ugliness to produce a beautiful dwelling?

Do you have dreams and visions that you've laid down because of life's disappointments?

CHAPTER FIVE
FOUNDATION

I'M IN NEED OF A GOD, THE BIG GUY OF THE TRIUNE CO-OP

I know that it sounds backwards to say I experienced the love of Jesus (Waymaker) and Helper (Holy Spirit) first, before I actually had a sit-down with God (the Big Guy). Remember, they are all part of the Trinity (Triune co-op) so even though I was learning from each of them, I was still experiencing all of them. Does that make sense?

God made it personal for me so I would be able to learn His many different ways and attributes. I'm not saying this is how your journey will begin in your life. Each one of us have our own walk that will specifically meet our needs according to God's plans for our future and destinies. I did, however, want to express again the impact that my realtor/mentor made on my life.

If you remember, I mentioned that in the beginning I felt like an orphan. I believe this is the sad reality for most of us because no one, not even our parents, can maneuver our spiritual path for us. They can plant seeds along the way but as we grow, we are on our own with God. We have to walk out our own salvation and, unfortunately, experiencing some bumps and bruises along the way are a part of it (the hard work).

As parents, we've had moments when we've cried buckets for our children's walks to straighten. At times, we've practically begged God to spare our children and we are simply at a loss about what to pray for next. If anyone hasn't told you today, "You did the best you knew how to raise your kids," I will. "You gave everything you have and it was enough."

From here on out, we have no choice but to trust in the grace of God to carry us the rest of the way. He is able to cover our inadequacies and downfalls completely and faithfully. And there is no such thing as going backwards in the kingdom. He is able to do exceedingly abundantly more than you could ever ask or think. The only thing He's requiring now is your full attention and your whole heart. He wants your "sold out" attitude that you will do whatever it takes to clean up and follow His lead.

Do we trust Him to raise our kids after we've raised them? Do we trust Him to clean us up so that we can see miracles, signs, and wonders? Do we trust Him when our grown children hit difficult trials?

I really believe that we are all coming into times where what has always worked for us no longer works. God is bringing us into deeper levels of trust where all we have is His Word to rely on. Maybe He's teaching us to pray differently—offensively rather than defensively. Maybe this is our opportunity to build prophetic words of redemption, love, forgiveness, and wholeness out of scriptures. When we run out of words, we can speak His Words. Maybe then we can watch Him move His hand mightily.

You have this, friend! God's not running out of miracles anytime soon. He's the master investor and He is committed to you and your family. He wants and desires redemption and reconciliation much more than you do. He's simply asking for your yielded heart in the process.

I thought of a time when my daughter was struggling and the Lord reminded me it's the hard times that drew me near to Him. He said, "How do you know I'm not using her loneliness to draw her near to me?"

We work so hard to protect our children from pain. But what if it's the pain that creates character in them so they can be all He's called them to be in the future? This is where we have to trust Him at a greater level. When we encounter His love, we feel adopted by Him in the spirit and we become His child. The Trinity is personal and loves relationships with each one of us.

When someone has an encounter with God's love and approval in his or her lives, no one can talk them out of that experience. When you are radically touched by His love, He stains you. You are forever changed. He made you for a relationship and connection with him. There's a spot that you fill in His heart, exactly like each of our children fill a spot in our hearts. There's a place in Him that can only be filled by you. He adores YOU!

As His child, life goes on and the journey takes on its own challenges and plot twists. We survive by Him feeding us milk, strengthening us slowly, and nurturing us one day at a time. Soon, we are translated from our orphan mindset into sons and daughters of the kingdom. We begin eating real food from His Word and we find ourselves beginning to speak life into those we care about. We feel ourselves becoming stronger day by day. He starts teaching us spiritual warfare and how to contend for the destinies of the broken. We begin to partner with Him and graduate from being His sons and daughters to mothers and fathers in the spirit, nurturing His orphans.

Urie and his precious wife, Amanda, were able to minister to the canyons of my heart, where there was a deficit left behind by my biological parents. They operated as my spiritual mother and father as they spoke life and purpose into my brokenness. This introduced me to a personal relationship with the Lord where I was then rescued from my orphan heart.

Their acts of kindness and obedience to God caused them to meet me right where I was. I didn't have to perform. I was

PART 1

vulnerable, ugly, and often a mess. But they chose to see me as the Heavenly Father sees me. The job of a spiritual parent is to guide people toward the true heavenly blueprint for their lives and purpose. Urie and Amanda earned my respect and honor because they didn't try to make me a mini version of themselves. They wanted me to look like Jesus.

It may have sounded strange to compare Urie to a realtor, but he helped me understand the spirit of adoption God could give me. He taught me I was no longer a foreigner in my land, but a pioneer who could make my dwelling here. I learned from his leading that I was not only a citizen of heaven, but I have an important part to play here on earth. He guided me to not only find my dwelling but to possess it, allowing God to uncover my inheritance and restore the years the locusts ate.

God knows everyone intimately and personally. The scriptures say, "But now, this is what the Lord says—he who created you, Jacob, he who formed you, Israel: 'Do not fear, for I have redeemed you; I have summoned you by name; you are mine'" (Isaiah 43:1).

We are seeing the enemy highjack and deceive God's people on massive and global scales. The confusion, decline of morals and values, and extreme brokenness are nothing more than identity theft (remember the bank vault). We are watching orphans run amuck because they don't know who they are or where they belong. Somewhere there was a breach and unauthorized transactions took place. The funds were depleted, the firewall was hacked, and the integrity of the person was compromised.

The Bible speaks of better things. "Before I formed you in the womb, I knew you, before you were born I set you apart; I appointed you as a prophet to the nations" (Jeremiah 1:5).

Each lost soul is known by the Creator since before they were knit together. When a mother and father in the spirit enter the picture, they are able to see orphans through God's eyes. Often earthly parents don't know how to meet the needs of their broken children because they've never dealt with their own brokenness. Does this mean they were failures? Absolutely not!

Things are typically caught, not taught. God is raising up an army of spiritual mothers and fathers who are not moved by the messiness of the orphans. They are not polluted by the judgments and accusations of family dynamics. They don't try to change them to suit their own needs or agendas. They lead them to God, the perfect Father. The orphan's cries are heard. They are finally given permission to be truthful, transparent, and vulnerable without condemnation, shame, and blame. Often, you will then see these children going back and setting their parents free. Now, that is true honor.

From a spiritual mother and father standpoint, the only caution I see is making sure to always point the orphans to the Creator who owns their heart. Ungodly soul ties can be easily formed when those we mentor develop a full dependence on us rather than the Lord. Remember, we are only to guide and direct those we mentor to the heavenly blueprint for their destiny and purpose. God is their true spiritual father.

God's grace works like gravity. You don't have to think about gravity. It's just a law of nature that happens supernaturally. When a spiritual mother and father have allowed God to do the preparatory work needed within their hearts, they develop equity to be able to minister to others. God's grace then flows supernaturally from the heavens down to the heart and reaches out, without us even thinking about it.

As your spirit knew Him before you were knit together, it is able to step forward and engage with the familiar message that your mentors are able to give. The orphans step forward and engage with the words of the spiritual mother and father because they are reminded of what they once knew before they were knit together.

You see, the enemy can do all he wants to steal the identity of that dear one, but there's one thing that can't be stolen: the fingerprints of DNA on the heart, left by the Father of Lights.

This precious gift of giving back to the broken what God has invested in you, isn't simply an honor—it's a requirement. This redemption isn't only about who is in your inner circle or within

PART 1

your own home. The earth groans for the sons and daughters to find their rightful place within the Kingdom of God and if you participate, you will be a part of the greatest story ever told.

It's time to meet the Big Guy of the Triune co-op. Are you ready? Let's go into the foundations.

I fell asleep among the trees and wild flowers and woke up with a sudden jolt. I heard His voice calling from the foundations of the house. "It's time to meet Me there." Oh, but I couldn't, I shouldn't, I won't! But He kept pulling on my heart. "Come on, it's time."

I was afraid of what we would uncover because of what I had been hiding in the deep places in the foundations. The ground had shifted from years of abandonment, and earth had been disrupted by failures and unfinished efforts.

The voice calling to me was different yet familiar. It was the softness of a lamb yet the roar of a lion combined. It stirred up intense fear and trembling within my heart. I laid there amongst the flowers for what seemed like an eternity, trying to discern if I was ready to go out and meet The Big Guy.

These foundations had suffered, having endured beatings by storms, torrential rains, and many outside offenses throughout the years. It was actually an absolute miracle that my house was able to stand at all with the foundation crumbling the way it was.

My thoughts were interrupted again.

"It's time. Come on, I'll meet you there."

Jeez, He sure is persistent. Obviously, He's more excited to dig into the foundations than I am. Maybe He already knows what's there. Hmmm, that's a thought. He is the expert architect and head honcho of the Triune co-op, after all. Before I could even think of another word, it slipped out of my mouth. "Okay, I'm coming."

I made it out to the clearing, on my way to the house, and there He stood. He looked at me with eyes I cannot explain in any words of my vocabulary. I felt loved yet afraid, protected yet exposed, quiet yet heard, glorious yet messy. How could one person bring out so many emotions in me at one time? It was as if He made me and knew every intricate detail of my entire being. I felt seen.

Without further hesitation, I quickly followed Him to take a look at my foundations. He spoke in authority yet expressed concern. "It looks as if your foundational issues have gone untreated for 48 years."

I thought, "I'm 48. What? Is He comparing the foundation to me?"

He answered, "Yes I know. But I knew you even before then."

I looked down. "What?" I thought. "He just read my mind."

He looked at me with deep tenderness. "I always do," He said.

He walked around to the other side of my foundation and pointed at a place where an actual rut had been created by the perpetual and consistent threats that had come against my infrastructure. What started as a minor crack had turned into a devastating and serious structural catastrophe. This rut compromised the value and overall health of my home. When the foundations shifted it affected not only the looks of my home outside but the strength and integrity of the inside.

If walls could talk. I could almost hear my house moaning and groaning. It wanted to fill up with happiness, a healthy outlook, and a lifetime of beautiful memories but it was simply too broken to be able to give anything out. My foundations couldn't protect me, let alone provide safety for an entire family or future generations.

My head hung in shame and I thought, "How did I let it get so out of hand?"

He answered my thoughts again by saying, "Dear one, no worries. Your foundation had never been given the proper support. It's clear by the way your house has settled that your foundation was compromised from the beginning and that's not all your fault. Come on, let's sit down and talk. You are overwhelmed and I want to partner with you and make this as easy as possible. Will you trust Me?"

Big Guy led me to that same spot among the trees and wildflowers that Waymaker and Helper loved. Ha ha, go figure. We sat down and He asked me what was on my heart. Niagara Falls gushed from my mouth! As if a tsunami had been awakened from its sleep, I began to share every ache and pain about my dwelling. He listened intently without judgment. And when I was all finished, He took a deep and a long sigh and said, "Thank you."

"For what?" I asked.

"I was just waiting for you to be honest," He said. "Now, how can we fix this?"

"I have no idea how to fix it. All of my life I've tried to fix it!" I blurted.

He shook His head as if to say He knew that already. "There's no shame or condemnation that you don't have it all together on this dwelling. Your realtor did well by providing you the services to get you started on your journey of owning what was rightfully yours," He said. "Waymaker showed you a greater path. He provided a way for you that was *paid in full* by His own blood and tears. Helper awakened you to hear the voice of the One who started the whole Triune co-op. That's me," He said with a big cheesy grin, "I'm the One."

I smiled back.

He had a sense of humor too and that ministered deeply to me because I've always had a playful side to me; I realized I have something in common with Him. Hey, maybe on this journey, I'll even be able to laugh at myself.

He took me by the hands and looked deeply into my eyes. "I'm the One who makes a way in the wilderness, dear one. I am able to create rivers in the desert. I am doing a new thing here. Now it springs forth; do you not perceive and know it and will you not give heed to it? Do not fear, for I have redeemed you. I have summoned you by name; you are mine. When you pass through the waters, I will be with you; and when you pass through the rivers, they will not sweep over you. When you walk through the fire, you will not be burned; the flames will not set you ablaze. You are precious and honored in my sight."

His words went deep into my core and I knew immediately that I was forever changed by His love and commitment to me.

We spent a good part of the day there under the trees. I kept thinking that at any moment, He would jump up, roll up His sleeves, and get into the dirty work of refurbishing my foundations, but He didn't seem to be in a big hurry. He wanted to spend time with me.

From time to time, He would smile at me and say, "Gosh, you're beautiful." At first it would make me uncomfortable and I would find my eyes immediately looking away from His eyes because it left me feeling so vulnerable. But I noticed as He continued to talk to me about my foundational corruption and weak areas, it became easier and easier to receive His words of affirmation.

Until I really took the time to talk and listen to Him, I hadn't realized how much shame and self-destructive behaviors I had. No wonder I found it so hard to rebuild my foundations. I needed to believe in myself and see me through His eyes. I found myself hanging on every word Big Guy said that day. His ability to explain things and captivate my heart was nothing short of a miracle.

Do you remember the trees I pruned in my garden with Helper? I suddenly realized that Big Guy was partnering with that process. You see, my soil was hard and dehydrated from the years I hadn't given myself nourishment from living water. I had shut myself down and allowed the hardening to take over because it hurt too much to go there. As He spoke to me that day, under those beautiful trees, I started to soften. As my soil rehydrated, the roots began to expose themselves again. Every root that had been trained to grow in the wrong direction, suddenly turned downward so that they could drink from the living water. Big Guy's words caused those roots to come alive. It appeared as if they were now planted by streams of water, yielding fruit in season, and with leaves that would not wither. My eyes were opened and I suddenly believed that my life would prosper.

PART 1

Then Big Guy took me by the hand to show me what our work had yielded that day. The closer we came to the foundation, the more nervous I became. What if I didn't listen enough? What if I wasn't a good student? What if my efforts were futile? I suddenly felt out of control and anxiety, doubt, and fear began to take over.

These negative emotions were always my "go to" in life. If I were a computer, these negative patterns were my default settings. I needed Him to help me reset my factory settings in my soul man. I desperately needed my soul man to be awakened to what my spirit man always knew since before the creation of the world.

He must have sensed my uneasiness because His firm hand closed in tighter around my fingers. I really felt out of control inside. I thought, "How will my foundation look any better? We didn't do anything but talk."

Again, He knew my thoughts. "Many things are accomplished when you talk to Me and allow Me to talk to you. I can erase in two minutes what you've carried for 48 years, simply by your yielding."

After a ten-minute walk, the house was finally in view and I chose to settle down by listening to His voice. I had no idea what we would see in front of us but my faith was stronger and my hand in His felt safe. He stepped forward with confidence and I found if I focused on the impressions that His feet made, my steps felt lighter and more secure.

I had to blink hard and then blink again and refocus my eyes to comprehend what was in front of me. I couldn't believe it. My foundations looked completely different. The cracks were gone, the holes were sealed, and my house was standing straighter. He looked at me with a proud Daddy's smile and said, "Good job!"

I smiled back and the most exhilarating and freeing wave of goodness I had ever experienced swept over me. It was a new day! It was never about my own works. It was about partnering with the One who could provide power, love, and a sound mind.

Big Guy seemed full of joy as He watched me come into a higher purpose. He literally skipped and danced all the way down to His vehicle. It was an amusing and hilarious sight to behold. It was as if fixing my foundations made His heart feel fulfilled as well. Perhaps He sees this as an opportunity for me to collaborate with Him in His business and vision. It would be quite rewarding to help people every day the way He does.

As I began to walk around my dwelling, I couldn't help but notice the atmosphere felt different. There was peace and I felt hope in my heart. I could sense a bright future coming my way and I didn't fear the unknown anymore. I looked down to see a single red rose popping up through the soil, so I picked it and smelled its beautiful fragrance. I sensed that Big Guy had left it for me as a reminder of His commitment and love for my dwelling. I finally felt the love of my Heavenly Father and there was no stopping me now. When I looked down, He had also left me a letter, folded neatly in the foliage. My hands shook as I unfolded it. What could He possibly want my heart to know now? His letter was written in the most beautiful handwriting I've ever seen.

"Blessed are the poor in spirit, for theirs is the kingdom of heaven.
Blessed are those who mourn, for they will be comforted.
Blessed are the meek, for they will inherit the earth.
Blessed are those who hunger and thirst for righteousness, for they will be filled.
Blessed are the merciful, for they will be shown mercy.
Blessed are the pure in heart, for they will see God.
Blessed are the peacemakers, for they will be called children of God.
Blessed are those who are persecuted because of righteousness, for theirs is the kingdom of heaven" (Matthew 5:3–10).
I love you dear one,
YOUR Heavenly Father

My heart feels so full.

PART 1

How do you see God? Ruling with an iron fist or loving and kind?

Do you trust God with your children and their destinies? Do you trust Him enough to allow them to walk through their own bumps and trials?

What lies have you believed about God?

Do you have a glimpse of the plans and purposes God has for your life?

Are there any orphans in your life to whom you feel led to minister God's love?

CHAPTER SIX

BASEMENT

I'M IN NEED OF A HELP MATE, MY DAVID

When I met my David, I wasn't expecting to find true love again. God had already done an amazing job captivating my heart and I honestly felt like I would be okay if I spent the rest of my years alone. I felt confident in the healing I had already walked out. The Lord created new identity and purpose in my life and I was blessed with a good job and able to provide well for my three children. However, I also knew that in order for me to operate in my fullest calling and use the giftings God gave me, I would need a strong covering. By no means is this meant to create pain for my single friends out there and again, our journeys all look different.

David and I met in a very unique way and there was an instantaneous prompting of the Holy Spirit that we were to be in each other's lives. I will never forget my first date with him in Roscoe Village. I came home and told my mother that I would be marrying him someday. I don't think she was ready to hear that! She had personally witnessed the destruction in my previous relationships and I'm sure she shuddered at the thought of me making this decision so prematurely. But one of our first conversations over dinner involved our thoughts on ministry. We both felt a strong encouragement of the Lord in our hearts to build the kingdom of God, and we both teared up as we experienced a kindred connection.

David had also been on a deep and life-changing journey with the Lord before he met me. God guided him faithfully in self-discovery, forgiveness, and redemption. He had also had childhood traumas to sort through and be healed. He also understood the impact of being raised in a home where the father didn't engage with his heart and the mother's control took away his masculinity and protection. He grew up carrying a pain that literally affected every area of his life. His father never, ever told him he loved him or believed in him and this offense against David's heart made it near impossible for him to thrive as a healthy man. His father then committed suicide when David was only in his twenties and this hole left him feeling vulnerable and unfulfilled.

When we talked, it was like dancing in the rain. It was fun and exciting. We finished each other's sentences, and it seemed like we were a perfect fit—hand in glove.

David asked me to marry him and because we wanted to live according to the Word, we began to search out pastors and mentors who could give us insight on divorce and remarriage. In light of how our marriages ended and after studying the Word thoroughly, we came away with the absolute knowledge that God was for us. But I still felt I needed a firm confirmation.

I was in the Amish taxi service business at the time and had picked up a load of 14 young girls who were attending a Christmas party that evening. The plan was to drop them off and then go back later to retrieve them and take them home. I couldn't help but notice a huge sign hanging on a building on one of the back roads where I traveled. The sign was lit up with the words, "Christ is the Answer!" After I dropped the girls off, I drove past the sign again before I headed home.

That night, I laid on my face before God on my living room floor. The kids were at their grandparents' house so I had the entire evening to myself. There I bared my heart and cried out for God to confirm what I believed He had put in my spirit concerning David. I told the Lord I was willing to lay all of my desires down and walk away from the relationship if He wanted me to. I cried until I had filled several kleenexes with my tears. I loved David very much but I loved God more and only wanted His will for my life.

Nine o'clock came along and it was time for me to head back to pick up the girls from their party. Friends, my heart was not prepared for what was about to happen. I rounded the corner on the familiar back road and was about to pass the building with the huge sign when something told me to look up again. I almost drove off the road when I witnessed with my very eyes what only God could do at that moment. There in front of me was the huge lit sign but the *H* had blown out. The sign now read, "Crist is the Answer!" David's last name was Crist.

Overwhelming joy and peace flooded my heart. I had to park my van and sit on the roadside to take in that moment of God's approval of our relationship. I literally felt the presence of the Lord fill my van. The weight of His glory was affirming and tangible. All I could do was cry with thanksgiving. I never doubted the decision again and we married the following March.

With all the healing we had already walked through on an individual basis, we were sure we would have a marriage made in heaven. But we soon learned that living in the same house together still touched some vulnerable places which the Lord had not yet healed. How many of you know that we are a work in progress? I'm convinced we never completely arrive into our full healing until we leave this earth and face our Maker. When we have unhealed places in our hearts, offenses within the home can trigger us pretty quickly. And God used

PART 1

our inadequacies, human mistakes, and fiery reactions to take us all to the next level.

It became plain and simple as I watched this thing play out in front of me. I saw that when we reacted in anger, frustration, hurt, or anything negative, it was an indication we needed to search deeper to discover what that offense had triggered within our emotions. If we were able to respond in love, kindness, and anything of goodness, you could clearly see where God had done a deep work previously and we were operating out of the heart of Jesus. Emotions and interactions became a barometer or gauge for me to see where we all still needed the help of a Savior or inner healing.

The first year was the hardest because David didn't only take on a woman but also a family of four. Three of us were girls so you can only imagine the river of estrogen that he was forced to swim in daily. He was a brave man to take on a woman with three children and when I look back to that time, I love him more today because he was willing. In many ways he saved us.

Inviting this precious man into our home gave us something we all needed desperately: healthy alignment and accountability. "Two are better than one, because they have a good return for their labor: If either of them falls down, one can help the other up. But pity anyone who falls and has no one to help them up" (Ecclesiastes 4:9–10).

Alignment and accountability in our home not only produced healthy sons and daughters, but it clearly taught us to be honest with each other about our feelings. When there isn't a safe and healthy place to process your emotions—no matter how ugly—families fall apart. Trauma and unhealed soul wounds are a breeding ground for disruption and adversity.

Transparency, when harnessed by the hand of the Lord, provides safety and success. Just as healthy alignment is desperately needed in a home, it is also needed within the church body. Just as the children and wives suffer if dad is out of God's order, so the church suffers if leaders are out of order. The husband represents to his wife what Christ represents to the church. Jesus laid His life down for the church. He died for it. David quickly came into the position of not only becoming our head but he developed a servant's heart.

An iron fist will provoke a family to anger but a tender servant's heart breathes life and blesses future generations. The church has done a good job of blessing people but the Holy Spirit wants to do more than bless people. He wants to equip them for a Spirit-led life. Remember, this is about God's business, not our agenda. Everything rises and falls on the health of the leadership. Alignment is everything. "Be strong and courageous. Do not be afraid or terrified because of them, for the Lord your God goes with you; he will never leave you nor forsake you" (Deuteronomy 31:6).

As a family we started to really pay attention to our triggers in response to others' actions. If we operated out of anything other than the character or nature of Christ, then we knew that God wanted to touch an unhealed place. We gave each other permission to share exactly what was on our hearts and it was up to the other person or people not to judge or condemn, but rather to listen.

Remember we cannot tell someone that what they feel is wrong because it is very real to them. If their feelings or opinions affected our hearts in a negative way, we would then take that opportunity to go to the Lord and ask Him to evaluate our dwelling. Ask not and receive not, correct? Sometimes we don't get the answers we need because we simply don't ask. Nine times out of ten, God would end up showing us an injustice or memory of something that happened in our past where we felt shut down, unheard, or unvalidated.

Even though we knew He'd never left us, it became a habit for us to ask the Lord, "Where were You during that offense when I was so wounded?" Without fail, He would faithfully show us a circumstance we may have forgotten about but He certainly hadn't. He would often give us or the kids a picture in our minds or hearts of where He was during that time. Seeing Him squashed the lie that we were never defended. It provided us an opportunity to issue forgiveness to the offender or ask for forgiveness for holding a grudge. We would then invite the love of Jesus to come in and we would ask for His blood to heal that broken area and make it as if it had never happened.

As we began to practice this as a family both corporately and individually, we began to see how we reacted a whole lot less and responded a whole lot more. We were able to respond in love, honor, and respect for the broken. We could validate their feelings and allow them to be heard. This practice was a gift from the Lord. We could now provide a safe place for each other's hearts. It also established a healthy foundation or platform for our children to grow from so they could go on and create healthy homes.

Sadly, this is a gift that is missing within the church. Too often, leaders are put on a pedestal and expected to be perfect. Leaders can also feel broken and defeated if they are not able to meet the expectations laid before them. Whether you are leading a home or a church, the best gift you can give God's people is the gift of vulnerability and transparency. Our ceiling becomes their floor. If we can show we are still very much in process and in need of a Savior daily, it will provide a safe place for those we lead to do the same with no condemnation.

We are constantly in between two colliding kingdoms. The kingdom of God wants to see us advance and succeed. The kingdom of darkness wants to see us fail and suffer. We must choose each moment which kingdom we will honor. We must choose each moment which kingdom we will serve when we are ministering to others, too. This isn't only about protecting our own hearts. This is about giving many hearts a kingdom advancement that aligns with destinies and purposes.

God's heart is truly to protect us from harm in our relationships. Sometimes, I feel people are too quick to blame Him when bad things happen but He is always good. We need to go after the enemy when bad things happen and using the name of Jesus is not only powerful, it's like sending fire into the enemy's camp!

David also learned in our marriage how to allow me to walk in my position of authority, as a daughter of the King, within our home. He gave me permission to hear the Holy Spirit for myself without judgement. What amazed me was that he often weighed my thoughts and revelations before the Lord for confirmation and many times came back to tell me I was correct.

I'll never forget a time when he was teaching children's church and the topic was hearing the Holy Spirit. He asked me to visit the classroom that day because he wanted to use me as an example. To my amazement, he announced before the children, "This is my wife and I brought her here to introduce you to someone who hears God. My wife hears the Holy Spirit more than anyone else I know in my life." Wow. WOW, WOW, WOW!

He recognized and honored my relationship with God. Honor paves the way to restoration. His words affected me deeply and somehow, they forever changed my ability to express my God thoughts with my husband. I don't hold back. I'm able to be completely up front with him on my spiritual journey. What a gift.

Women tend to be more emotional by nature and are often misrepresented in the church because of that. I would like to submit to you that tenderness and emotions are not a weakness. Jesus was a prime example as He often cried and expressed Himself with emotions. His horrible death and sacrifice were not merely so men could rule—they were also for the freedom of both men and women alike to operate in their God-given potential.

Women are far from weak. If there was ever a man to question that, I would encourage them to give birth to a baby. However, clearly men are stronger in stature and are able to do many things that women can't physically accomplish. My point is this, "So God created mankind in his own image, in the image of God he created them; male and female he created them" (Genesis 1:27).

PART 1

He created THEM—both of them—to be just like Himself. We all carry our own unique giftings. One gift does not diminish another. They are meant to work together for the benefit of the body of Christ. Clearly women represent the feminine side of God and men represent the masculine side of God. David and I have learned the value of honoring one another's gifts. We also recognize we don't truly need each other to be made whole. We each go to God first for our full value and affirmation. Anything we give to each other aside from that is the icing on the cake, but we don't *need* each other.

We live our lives separated unto the Lord so, when we come together, we are able to hear one another by the Spirit. We trust one another's discernments and choices. We partner with each other's giftings and anointings. We work together like peanut butter and jelly. Our identities are not *each other* but *God* first, so we seem to flow with ease.

Women are able to do so many wonderful things but birthing and bringing lives into this world is one of the best miracles she can provide in the natural. She is also able to birth and bring life in the spiritual if she is loved and honored well. A man who loves his wife well, gives her permission to be the best version of herself—her God-given self. When he serves her well, she will in turn desire to serve him well. It's a cycle of beauty and a life that continues to breed healthy relationships in the future.

David will tell anyone that listens, "My wife knows the voice of the Lord." He has grown to love, admire, and glean from my ability to hear the Holy Spirit and this spurs me on to press in and develop my relationship with God even more.

It's time to go into the basement of the house. Oh, what will we find?

Getting my foundation fixed gave me hope for the scary basement. This part of my journey seemed easier because I'd married during the last year and I wouldn't have to clean up this mess alone.

When we took inventory of our surroundings, there was strong evidence of the stress, shifting of the walls, and damage to every area affected by our unhealthy foundations. Here we stood, looking at not only my walls, or his walls, but our walls combined. It's amazing that this house was still standing at all. How in the world would we support and operate a healthy home with these visible signs that there was still brokenness?

The Triune co-op all showed up that day to help us evaluate the damage. All three were so wonderful, guiding us in our emotional investments and also our financial decisions. Helper spoke up and penetrated the depths of our hearts with the words, "My strength is made perfect in your weaknesses."

The next season of our lives was spent in that nasty basement, every single day. It was the most painful yet glorious experience in our marriage. There we worked together to establish a healthy home, not only for us but also our children, grandchildren, and their children. We grew to love the process because we trusted the Ones who held us.

When any conflicts would arise, Waymaker would sit us down and tell us the story of His sacrifice again. If He could redirect our own selfish desires and agendas back to the price He paid, we were able to calm back down again and re-engage in the journey. Big Guy showed us there were rooms in our hearts and house where we clearly had not allowed Him to be a guest in our home. Yet there were other rooms where the windows were brightly lit by His light because we'd allowed Him to take up residence there.

He encouraged us that it would be okay to take our time as we allowed Him into each space. But He was sure to affirm us that the quicker we heeded His direction, the safer our home would feel.

As my husband and I continued to shore up the basement of our home, things came up that were terribly uncomfortable and hidden. Some of these things were painful and hard enough to talk to each other about, let alone the Triune co-op. Waymaker dropped in many times to help guide our hearts and often reminded us He holds the keys to unlock every prisoner held captive. He would talk to us about our inheritance that He left us; He would slip the keys into our hands and say, "Go, unlock those doors. I'm here and I've given you every gift I have so that you can be more than conquerors." That encouragement alone would take our minds off of ourselves and back onto Him again.

It was amazing. The Triune co-op permanently walked closely alongside each of us to provide coaching, direction, instruction, and counsel in our life journey. They never tired. It didn't matter how many times we called upon their names, they were always there. They said they would abide with us forever and they weren't kidding.

My husband and I learned a valuable lesson as we were rebuilding, which goes back to Matthew and the Beatitudes. When we stopped being poor in spirit, we found ourselves slipping backwards in the kingdom-building. It was a gift to admit our absolute and total dependence on God's spirit to refresh us daily.

If we felt sad and down, we never forgot the Waymaker's example of compassion and we provided comfort for each other's weakness.

If we stayed humble with one another by taking on the character and nature of Christ, we felt the approval of the Trinity and inherited goodness—for ourselves and for our children.

We learned the importance of staying hungry and thirsty for righteousness. We knew it was wrong to stomp our feet and demand we were right, and learned to rather open ourselves to the possibility that we could be wrong. This kept us hungry and thirsty, and by looking to God for the approval of our actions rather than to each other, we found ourselves satisfied.

When one would extend mercy to the other and choose to see the good in any given situation, then mercy was given back when that person needed it the most. We learned to help one another grow in our faith by speaking words of affirmation and life.

The more purity and wholeness we spoke to and about each other, the more we were able to see God move on our behalf. We encouraged one another to be peacemakers and not peacekeepers. We had both grown up in homes where the truth wasn't freely spoken and that had taught us to perform and do whatever we could to keep the peace. But often it was at our expense or the expense of others because then the truth was never spoken. So, by encouraging one another to be peacemakers, we were giving permission to speak the truth in love, for the truth will set us free. Being vulnerable and open to the Big Guy is what brought us out of our orphan mindsets and into being children of God. If He expected the truth from us then how much more does He expect us to speak the truth to one another?

My husband and I also learned we wouldn't always be accepted by others. Jesus went to the cross perfect and blameless, yet people hated Him and wanted Him dead. If He couldn't fight hatred then what made us think that we could? However, He promises us that we will inherit the kingdom of heaven, in spite of the cases being built against us, if we are choosing to live in His glory.

We have an audience of One, friends. We are given one life and that life is expected to fulfill the plans and purposes He created us for. Do not allow anyone or anything to steal your Godly inheritance. It's important to hear the words, "Well done my good and faithful servant."

I'm so excited to go upstairs now but I think our journey ends here. I'll pass you on to Barb. I trust she can guide your heart the rest of the way. Go Pioneer! Go embark on the adventure of a lifetime that awaits you. May you be blessed of the Lord and find the plans and purposes you were created for. We want your dwelling to flourish with the fruit that He intended. Go and be about your Father's business.

PART 1

Do you ever feel triggered by your circumstances?

Are you able to see where your triggers touch unhealed places within your heart?

Does your spouse or significant other give you permission to be real, raw, and honest about your feelings?

Does your church leadership show that it's ok to be vulnerable, giving you permission to be in process?

Are you able to allow the Trinity into each room of your home/heart?

BASEMENT

  I love helping others get freed from their past and to advance from there toward their full potential and destiny. Taking my free *Freedom Assessment* is a great place to start. Head here to take the free assessment plus gain access to all my free resources:

https://www.angelacrist.me/free-resources

Angela Crist,
Helping you *Go Deeper So You Can Grow Higher*

PART 2

Lighting up the Present

CHAPTER SEVEN
RECOGNIZE

THE NEED FOR A CONSULTATION/ DESIGNER

Oh, my simple life . . . It started off unassuming, a bit obscure and somewhat uneventful. I remember telling a friend about my upbringing over coffee one day and she said, "Oh my, I'm sorry. That's so sad." Her response caught me off guard. You see, I have never really thought of my life as being sad. I knew it hadn't been easy at times, but it was a good life; I had learned to be grateful for it all.

I was the youngest of three girls. My oldest sister had cerebral palsy. So, as a kid she struggled to walk and talk clearly. As time went on, she needed a walker and eventually she spent the latter part of her life in a wheelchair.

She was 14 years older than me and even though I was much younger, I was a fierce protector of her. As a small child, I would try to intercept the stares of those who saw her as different. I wanted them to see her as I did—VALUABLE! It made me sad for her and my heart was tender for the challenges she faced daily.

However, she had an incredible impact on my life. She was a sweet soul. Even though her speech was slurred and her body twisted, she smiled more than anyone I had ever met. Not only was she full of joy, she was my teacher. She taught me to have deep compassion and acceptance of others. I learned we are all alike; every human heart seeks love, kindness, understanding and respect, despite our outward conditions.

I'll never forget the day her words changed me forever. I was getting ready to go out with friends when she said something that stopped me in my tracks. She leaned back in her wheelchair and in her broken speech she said, "Barb's so lucky!"

That really bothered me. As a clueless and self-centered teenager, I snapped back. "What? And why would you say that?"

She continued, "Barbie gets to go places, Barbie gets to have a boyfriend, Barbie gets to get married, Barbie gets to have babies."

She didn't say it in anger or frustration, but simply as a profound and painful self-realization for the both of us. I stood there stunned, knowing that every word she just said was true.

She felt it; I felt it.

I was the one who could talk clearly, walk without effort, and build a life of my own, not because I had done anything right or that she had done anything wrong; it was simply our respective portions in this life. The question I would ask myself often after that encounter is, "Why me?" How could I make the most of the tremendous gifts I had been given?

My middle sister was, well, let's say I wanted to be exactly like her. She was eight years older than me and I followed her around like a shadow, a lost puppy of sorts. Some of my most vivid memories of her were yelling from upstairs, "Mom, Dad, get her out of my room!" But as the years went on, the age difference seemed to slowly disappear and we became the best of friends and closest allies.

My mother was a stay-at-home mom. She was gentle, meek, very soft spoken, and always doing for others. My dad owned a saw mill along with our family farm. You could easily find me by his side at any given time. He made life fun. I remember laughing and joking as he taught me how to work hard.

Often in the evenings, I would go out to his workshop and do odd jobs for him. I'm sure I wasn't much help but he sure made me feel like I was needed. At the end of every evening, he would always ask me the same question. "Would you like me to pay you or take you to *Save 4*?" which was a little mom-and-pop convenience store down the road. There, I would be allowed to get a little brown paper bag and select my favorite penny candy from the huge assortment of canisters. Actually, I don't ever remember taking the money; I would simply grin from ear to ear with my chubby little cheeks and off we'd go to *Save 4*. You see, I was his sidekick and he was my best friend, my hero!

I'll never forget one summer night at the age of 12, I was getting ready for bed and I wanted so badly to listen to the radio my sister had in her room. It was my oldest sister, the one with disabilities and she was not one to share anything, at least not without a fuss. So, I quietly asked my dad for permission and he nodded, "Yes," and then from across the room he tossed me a pillow and winked. "Here," he whispered, "cover it up with this and save the peace!" We both laughed. So, quietly I took the radio, covered it with the pillow and went running up the stairs. I distinctly remember wanting to run back down and give him a hug and kiss good night like I had done every other night, but I thought no, I've made a clean break without my sister realizing I had the radio. I was pretty proud of myself.

The next morning, I woke up to my mother sitting on the end of my bed, which I thought was strange. My mom simply said, "Daddy's gone." In my confusion, I sat up and said, "Where did he go?" There was silence and then after a long and uncomfortable moment, she said once again, "Honey, daddy's gone."

PART 2

As my mind wrestled to make sense of her strange statement, I sat quietly, frozen in disbelief. As my mind processed it, at that very moment in time my entire world caved in on me; nothing would ever be the same. I sat for what seemed like hours, trying to wake up from this nightmare.

Dad had a massive heart attack that night as I slept. The emergency squad had come with lights and sirens in the middle of the night in an attempt to revive him. I had slept through it all. I believe it was by God's grace I didn't have to witness the trauma of that night. My dad was only 51 years old and now he was gone, gone forever! My father, my friend, my protector—gone. As the painful months passed, we did the only thing we could: we rallied together as we tried to pick up a million broken pieces, and pressed on as best we could.

Shortly after the loss of my earthly father, I met my heavenly Father. He became my confidant, my protector, and over the years my Daddy. I am pretty sure the minute my dad got to heaven, he had a conversation with the Father about the little girl he had left behind and how she would need a Dad such as Him to help navigate the rough waters I would face through this journey called life.

"But may the righteous be glad and rejoice before God; may they be happy and joyful. Sing to God, sing in praise of his name, extol him who rides on the clouds; rejoice before him—his name is the Lord. A father to the fatherless, a defender of widows, is God in his holy dwelling" (Psalms 68:3–5).

During my teenage years, God was faithful to guide me and keep me from a lot of heartache. I felt His protection and often went to Him for guidance with questions I would have asked my dad if he was still on this earth. Because of that, I believe it was easier for me to trust the Father's intentions for my life. As I grew up and went deeper in my faith, I learned more and more about Jesus. I learned of His extraordinary love for me and how He could relate to my broken heartedness, my betrayal, and my need for unconditional love. Not only was He my savior, but He had become my best friend. He was the one

I would share my deepest thoughts and feelings with, along with my hopes and dreams.

As much as I believed in the Trinity, I must say the Holy Spirit was a bit of a mystery to me. I grew up in a Mennonite Church. Little was mentioned of the Holy Spirit—at least that was true in the church I attended. Nor did I hear about how His immense power and comfort was made available to those who decided to partner with Him. It's sad to say, but in my ignorance, I missed out on so much valuable time with Him, the lover of my soul. However, He has been faithful to take me by the hand and uncover the giftings that have been so carefully placed within me, giftings to help others.

It has been incredible to watch His plans unfold as He so carefully nurtures and expands my heart. It thrills me when I feel His love flow through me to touch others! He has become my teacher and I have become His student. It's through His eyes I can see His deep compassion, acceptance, and the unique plan for each one of us.

My heart comes alive as I witness the Father, Son, and Holy Spirit take me deeper and deeper into their presence. I believe I have been uniquely placed here to help you partner with the Great Designer to create an indescribably beautiful place for Him to dwell and operate.

I have learned everything He does is by design. He is highly creative, but yet He follows an ordered process. He began to enlighten my heart as He showed me the correlation of what I do in the *physical* is what He does in the *spiritual*, filling my mind daily with detailed word pictures as He poured truth deep within me.

He would whisper to me as I spent time with Him in the secret place. What an unbelievable place this is. It's a place of great security, peace, and understanding. I have spent many nights there.

"He will cover you with his feathers, and under his wings you will find **refuge**; his **faithfulness** will be your **shield** and **rampart** (Psalm 91:4).

PART 2

When I am in His presence, I am often overcome with emotion. It is inexplicable to be known, to be truly known and accepted at this level. There, He assures me of my worth to Him, for He is the one who formed me and created me in a way that brings Him joy. You see, I am His masterpiece, highly valued and meticulously handcrafted.

"The word of the Lord came to me, saying, 'Before I formed you in the womb I knew you, before you were born I set you apart; I appointed you as a prophet to the nations.' 'Alas, Sovereign Lord,' I said, 'I do not know how to speak; I am too young.' But the Lord said to me, 'Do not say, "I am too young." You must go to everyone I send you to and say whatever I command you. Do not be afraid of them, for I am with you and will rescue you,' declares the Lord" (Jeremiah 1:4–8).

He has formed me to be creative and to see beauty in all things as He does. We all reflect Him through different facets of His being. Over the years, He has chosen to speak to my heart through parables. In the following pages I will share some of those with you in the hope it will bring you into a deeper understanding of how incredible He is.

The Father desires a relationship with us, so He graciously speaks our specific language. What do I mean by that? He formed every last detail of who we are and He comes to us from the Holy of Holies to communicate with us, but in such an intimate manner that we might understand His love for us in the deepest way possible.

So come with me and let's allow the God of the Universe to design our hearts in a way that will honor His mighty presence.

This is Life by Design.

I have been doing design work for years now; it's a part of who I am and it's sown into the fabric of my identity. I see endless possibilities—the treasure in the trash, the beauty in the ashes. It has become quite evident to me that what I possess is a gift because it's something that flows through me, not from me.

I'm a chip off the old block. You see I've come to think like my Father; He has always seen endless possibilities in me. He found the treasure in my trash. Not so long ago, my life was so full of trash there was enough to fill a dumpster or two. I will never forget how He got on His hands and knees next to me as we looked through the rubble of my life for something—anything—that could be salvaged. I never found much because my eyes were so full of tears it was hard for me to see clearly.

He was always finding the valuable pieces. He would be so excited to show them to me as He painstakingly cleaned them off and made them shine brighter than they did before. I would say, "That was in my rubble? I didn't even know it was mine." He would smile and say, "Oh, it's always been there; isn't it wonderful?" I would smile a little bit more each time He found another piece of my life that could be restored.

It was a slow process, but He never once left. He kept working even when I was sleeping. He was so committed to finding every last treasure of mine. He even collected the ashes and made the most beautiful masterpiece from them. To this day, I don't know how He did it, but it is now displayed proudly in the entrance of my heart.

In the coming chapters, I will walk you through the same process I use in the physical for my design work, while showing you how it parallels what God is doing in the spiritual to design our hearts. He is preparing a beautiful place for His Spirit to dwell. So, get ready for renovation, transformation, and off-the-hook *before* and *afters*!

STEP 1

RECOGNIZING THE NEED FOR A CONSULTATION

I decided to ask the Great Designer to do a complete makeover on my life. By this time, He had gained my complete trust and working with Him was wonderful. His portfolio was unbelievable and His referrals were impeccable. He did not have one unsatisfied client; can you believe that? So, I quickly scheduled a consultation with Him. He was prompt to get back to me and said He was very excited for the opportunity.

Our first meeting was interesting, even though I was a little nervous about what He might think of the place. He said He merely wanted to look around a bit, maybe get a tour from me. He was gracious and respectful. He didn't seem to be bothered by the mess or the dirt on my floors. And He didn't demand to enter any room I wasn't ready to show Him. "No worries," He said, "we'll take one room at a time."

He did ask me, however, what I liked about each room and also what I didn't like. He seemed curious about what I thought was functioning or serving me well. I thought that was an interesting question and it really made me think.

It thrilled me when He asked about my own personal style. You know, what colors energized me, what type of things brought me joy. He wanted me to share my vision and my dreams with Him. I could tell He really wanted the place to reflect my deepest desires and longings. By the time we were finished, I was so very excited! I could tell He understood me, He got me. I knew His plan would be far better than anything I could imagine or achieve myself.

I was ready to get started, even though He told me I would have a considerable amount of work to do. I was ready for the challenge and the changes that would take place within me. He said He would partner with me and direct me through the whole process. Then, He mentioned how He would be scheduling people to come at the perfect times to help me with particular jobs. He assured me He would be personally assisting me with any of the heavy lifting or deep cleaning that would be needed along the way. Isn't that awesome? I have never heard of another designer offering such a service.

The first step to any change is **recognizing** the need for it, whether it be in our homes or in our lives. My phone doesn't often ring until there is a design dilemma or a problem my clients cannot figure out on their own. When I show up, I am promptly shown what is wrong and asked a myriad of questions as they look on and expect an immediate answer.

How often do we do that with God? We tend to call Him when we are stuck and then we become frustrated when He doesn't provide us with a quick answer or solution. Are we willing to have Him look over our entire life and come up with a plan that fulfills His purpose for our lives? Or are we simply looking for a quick fix?

Personally, I rarely give answers on the spot; I first gather information from the homeowner before I can begin to devise the best plan for them. I ask questions like how much are they willing to invest in the design? What rooms do they think need a change and why? Are they willing to do some of the work themselves? Will they allow others to assist them? How open will they be to my suggestions? All super-important and telling questions.

You see I can devise the most incredible plan for them, but they must work with me to see it through to its completion. They will also need to trust me and what I have planned for them, even when they cannot envision it for themselves.

We walk through a similar process with God. More times than not, we will wonder what He is up to and have to trust His wisdom without the finished end in sight. Oh, my friend, it is a wild and wonderful adventure when you allow Him to carry out His creative masterplan for your life.

The process I take people through consists of many personal choices and selections along the way. This takes time and much direction from me as I guide them and keep them on track to honor the ultimate design plan. Sometimes, clients will start buying things on their own without considering scale, style, or even color at times! Selections like these can be costly to a well laid out plan. At a minimum they slow the process down and cause unnecessary chaos, frustration, and confusion to what we are trying to achieve.

PART 2

Please don't misinterpret what I'm saying. I want all my clients to ultimately make their own decisions, but they must be made within specific guidelines that fall within our agreed-upon design plan. For instance, if they desire a farmhouse vibe and I am helping them create that, there will be perimeters to guide us. Let's say over the weekend they come across a huge furniture sale and find a couch for an unbelievably good deal. Sound familiar? They decide to quickly purchase it without checking with me or referring back to the original plans. Why? Because the price and color seem perfect. However, the scale and style were wrong. It's far too big for the space and the style was ultra-contemporary. This one poor decision can ruin the entire design plan for the room.

This is not unlike what we do when God is helping us design a beautiful life. We will be making many important decisions along the way, like who we will choose for a spouse. If we desire to serve and please God, we must partner with Him. It is dangerous to make careless or big decisions without Him.

Sometimes people make decisions for a spouse like that couch purchase. Remember, it was almost a good fit. It may sound something like this: "He said he was a Christian; he sure did look the part. I knew he didn't like going to church, but I assumed eventually he would join me. I mean, it's not exactly what I was looking for in a man, but the relationship seemed comfortable and I thought choosing him was a safe enough bet." Crazy talk, but we make decisions like that when we aren't diligent about referring back to the best plan God has for us.

What happens when we realize it's not a good fit? Many times, we complain about how things look around us and how different our life turned out from what we had imagined. Even though we were instrumental in choosing and creating our current surroundings.

If this has happened to you, don't despair; it has happened to all of us to some degree. Our personal selections can be costly at times, even life-altering, but the great Designer is always ready to partner with us as we recognize, remove, repurpose, redeem, and realize all He has planned for us in His great design.

Take comfort in His ability to create a plan for your life, to keep you on track and if need be, get you back on track. Nothing is too difficult for Him.

"'For I **know** the plans I have for you,' declares the Lord, 'plans to **prosper** you and **not to harm** you, plans to give you **hope** and a **future**'" (Jeremiah 29:11).

"And we know that in all things God works for the **good** of those who love him, who have been called according to his purpose" (Romans 8:28).

"I will **instruct** you and **teach** you in the way you should go; I will **counsel** you with my loving eye on you" (Psalm 32:8).

"**Trust** in the Lord with all your heart and **lean not on your own** understanding; in all your ways submit to him, and he will make your paths straight" (Proverbs 3:5–6).

And your **DESIGN** will be beautiful!

PART 2

DESIGN STEP 1

Let's first RECOGNIZE the areas we want to work on in our home and life. As we prepare for the consultation, list below those areas.
What do you like about your home/surroundings?
What do you like about yourself/life?
What areas are functioning/serving you well in your home?
What areas are functioning/serving you well in your life?
Share your vision, style, and dreams for your home.
Share your vision, hopes, and dreams for your life.

CHAPTER EIGHT
REMOVE

THE UNREDEEMABLE COLLECTION

Isn't it good to step back and look at your life as a whole? What do I mean by that? Well, often we only focus on what is not working in our lives, and that can be overwhelming.

When we begin to identify the areas of our life that are functioning well and bringing us joy, it brings our best design plan into focus. That focus gives us the clarity and ability to remove those things that no longer belong in our new design.

When I first arrive at a new client's home, I see a house full of possessions and collections. Collections are not always pretty pieces in a corner cabinet, but they do indeed help tell their owner's story. They vary greatly from home to home. They may include a painting by a three-year old grandchild or a tribal mask from a far-away country purchased on a once-in-a-lifetime trip. These possessions are everywhere; some are beautiful, some are broken, some have great meaning, and some are useless. But how can we determine what stays and what goes?

PART 2

We start with the vision, hopes, and dreams the client has for the house and we identify the treasures. We certainly don't scrap everything, but we must begin to remove those things that have no redeemable value to the new design. Even though these items may appear quite obvious to many of us, people can have a difficult time letting go of them for a variety of reasons. However, this step is vital in beginning your own personal redesign.

Come with me on mine!

STEP 2

REMOVING THE UNREDEEMABLE COLLECTION

The next time we talked, He showed me a glimpse of the plan. I loved all His ideas but thought I may need to get rid of some of the old stuff to make room for all the beautiful pieces He showed me could be mine. Somehow, He read my mind and said, "You're correct; this is the stage where we need to REMOVE what is not working for you, things that could be holding you back from your best design."

I knew He was right. Come to think of it, He had helped me years previously to remove an ugly old piece. It was huge and took up half the room. It was given to me by those who had hurt me most in my life and it was loaded with unforgiveness and abandonment issues. I struggled to move that thing out of there, with no luck on my own. I remember making many calls to His office pleading for direction. He always took time to speak with me and He was incredibly patient. He often directed me to the wonderful step-by-step instruction book He wrote for me some 2000 years ago. (I still refer to it often.)

I must admit it was a struggle at times, but inch by inch we moved that piece until it was no longer in my dwelling. Its removal forever changed my space, which inspired me to be

REMOVE

willing to do the hard work of removing the other things that were no longer serving me. So, I asked for His honest opinion on what else needed to go.

As we strolled through my room, the Designer brought my attention to an old piece—a dresser—standing in the corner.

I said, "Oh, that old thing is heavy. I'm not even sure what's in there; it's been handed down to me from past generations."

I cringed inside and wondered if I should get rid of it. I mean, wouldn't that be a bit shameful? After all, it's been in the family as long as I can remember. Don't get me wrong, I didn't like anything about it but it was familiar and had always been stuck in that dark corner.

The Designer encouraged me to take a look inside, after which I could decide if it stayed or went. As I walked closer to it, I wondered how old it was and how it had ended up in my possession.

I slowly opened the top drawer and religiousness began to fall out of it. What in the world is that doing in there? I quickly picked it up and placed it back into the drawer, secretly hoping my Designer hadn't seen what it contained.

As I cautiously slid the next drawer open, a foul stench rolled out. What is all of this? It was stuffed full of shame and judgement. That was unsettling, to say the least. Who would keep things like this tucked away? I was taken aback by the terrible contents of this small dresser.

There was one last drawer to open. Honestly, I was hoping it would be empty, but it wasn't. In fact, I was shocked and horrified by what I saw there. Looking in, I found a single item. What and why is there a muzzle in here? My mind raced for a reasonable answer, but found none.

As I peered deeper into the drawer, I saw an old, yellowed piece of paper. It was folded neatly with the word *INSTRUCTIONS* written across it. I opened it carefully and read: *To be used ONLY in case of an EMERGENCY.* It went on to say: *If one among us refuses to conform and cannot be quieted*

PART 2

with the shame and judgment provided in the drawer above, this must be used before they find their VOICE.

Needless to say, I was speechless, saddened, and then angry about what I had uncovered. This dresser is what had been handed down to me by my ancestors? And to think I had kept it for so many years, never fully aware of its contents. If it were not for the Designer bringing it to my attention, I would surely have handed that stinky old piece down to my own children. The thought of it enraged me.

I can only describe it as a Holy Anger. My voice became louder and stronger and vibrated from within me as we moved that ugly old piece out.

I said, "What is happening, great Designer?"

He smiled like I had never seen Him smile before and said, "We are cleaning house and making room for all things beautiful!"

Oh, how I took comfort in His reassuring words and the things He gave me that day. Where shame and judgement once were, He left a gorgeous piece full of Honor and Mercy, which smelled like spring. It was fresh and life-giving and it made me want to use my voice that was once silenced, to sing His praises.

My place was looking remarkably different already. Then He presented me with the most heartfelt gift I have ever received: a beautifully framed picture of me and Him. I'm not even sure when it was taken. It was the most incredible thing! When you turned it, the image changed. If I held it one way, we were laughing; another turn and it looked as if we were in deep conversation; another slight turn showed Him crying with me; yet another and He was praying over me as He kissed my head.

What an incredible gift. I was speechless. I loved it so much, I didn't know what to say. He grinned as He tried not to cry from emotion and said, "It's to replace religiousness; it's us, it's our relationship." And then He said quietly, "I paid the ultimate price for that piece, but it was so worth it to spend those moments with you."

REMOVE

I wept as I admired its beauty. He hung His head as a tear rolled down His cheek. "I'm so glad you like it, my child," He said. Somehow, He was far more than my Designer from that day forward.

Time passed and I was enjoying my surroundings much more without that heavy old piece in my corner. Its absence had made room for all the new treasures the Designer had left for me.

As I was admiring the work we had done, I received an unexpected "package" from a friend. It was actually a text message. At first glance I was confused as to why she would have sent it to me. Was it a gift? You see it was spattered here and there with little hearts, smiley faces, and a few exclamation marks. At first glance, it appeared to be a kind gesture. But slowly, as I opened the text, a strange smell arose which sickened me. Why would a friend send me such a package? I honestly think she expected me to place it in my new, clean room. But why?

As I was contemplating what to do next, I caught another whiff of that awful smell. It seemed so familiar. Where had I smelled that before? Suddenly, I realized it was the same smell that had oozed out from that old dresser my ancestors had left me.

Her text questioned my new-found boldness to stand for what I believed. Ever so kindly, she suggested I may want to keep those sorts of convictions tucked away. You know, toned down a bit. After all, who did I think I was to speak out on such matters? Where had I heard this before?

Immediately, in my mind I could see the muzzle being removed from the bottom drawer. Oh no, I will not put that on! What should I do? Who should I call? How would I respond to the sender of this package?

I quickly called the Designer and like always, He listened intently. He did not seem surprised that I had received such a package. I pleaded with Him to tell me what to do next. "What do I do with this package?"

PART 2

His first reply was strange and caught me off guard. He asked me if I was going to keep the offense that came with the package. He said it was totally up to me. I pondered that for a long moment. I had been so focused on the strong smell of shame and judgement. I knew I wouldn't accept the muzzle back into my clean home, but I totally missed the offense so perfectly packed inside that it was almost invisible.

I didn't understand.

The Designer said, "That's what happens most of the time in these situations. It's actually the most destructive thing in those types of packages. Many will not accept the package as truth because of the strong smell that accompanies it, but they will strangely feel like they have no choice but to keep the offense."

He reminded me that the offense was very similar to the unforgiveness we'd moved out years ago. It too takes hold in the damp, dark places which are out of sight, and will grow insidiously behind the walls of your dwelling. It's exactly like mold; it will begin to give off a deadly toxin that will permeate the air and eventually destroy all within its reach.

Well, that shook me up a bit. What was I to do with all of this? I mean, a friend had sent it to me and I couldn't just ignore it. As I discussed this matter with my Designer, He shared a secret with me. You see, He too knows my friend and it sounds like He also does work for her on occasion. He told me she has a similar old chest that sits in the corner of her room. It was also handed down from past generations and every once in a while, she draws from the contents of those drawers and sends them to people—a regifting of sorts.

He said, "She hasn't completely moved that piece out of her dwelling yet. But with my help, she has been purging many other useless items. I am confident in due time she will allow me to help her move that ugly old piece out too."

He went on to say, "So, would you allow me to take that offense from you? In fact, I would like to take the whole package if you'll allow me. I don't want you to keep it and I certainly don't want you sending it back to her. I mean, that would totally interfere with the design I'm trying to do at her place."

I thought for a minute and said, "Absolutely! Thank you." Wow, what a considerate and wise Designer.

So, I agreed, even though it felt unnatural not to keep it for myself. He then went on to give me the perfect words to share with her so as not to slow down her design process or mine. It was a great reminder to me that He has a special interest in *every* job He is working on, not only mine.

The Removal Process is key in developing a beautiful design. This step cannot be skipped and is a great place to start when needing more clarity and direction. Normally, people know what pieces need to go and are looking for guidance as to how to replace it with something better. Other pieces are smaller and much more difficult to detect, but can cause havoc in a space. However, there are times when it becomes difficult for them to see or even admit to the pieces that are no longer working because they have simply become comfortable with the familiar. It can take patience and time for them to see the different options available to them.

That's where I come in. I give them vision for something better and brighter along with the tools they will need to remove it. Much like God does in our lives. He begins to unfold His plan for our lives and it is easier to get on board when we realize the possibilities. However, this can be more challenging for those who don't fully trust their Designer's vision or motivation.

Many people think if they have had something passed down to them, they must keep it. This is not true and it's a recipe for disaster when we hold on to that which depletes us. How about a bad temper that has been passed down? Have you ever heard someone say, "It's the family I come from; we're all hot heads and there was always yelling in our house." My question is, how is that working for you? Do you personally want to hold onto it? It doesn't have to stay and can surely be replaced with something far better and more useful.

PART 2

Some people insist on keeping pieces that don't serve them well and they admittedly do not even like because of the investment they have made. This sounds a bit irrational when keeping it will have a negative effect on what we are trying to accomplish. This could be likened to a relationship that no longer works or is destructive, but yet they feel they must keep it because of the valuable time they have invested in it. I'm not talking about walking away from a marriage or a family because it's difficult—that is a covenant that was made not only between you and your spouse, but God. It may need repurposed and restored, which God is a pro at doing. Rather, I'm referring to friendships or other relationships that are not life-giving and which are consuming valuable space in your life's design.

The reasons can vary, but by identifying what no longer works or brings you joy is paramount in loving your room or your life again. I'm not sure about you, but this excites me. Simply by eliminating things in our life we can vastly improve it.

I have clients who don't use certain rooms of their home because of the way they make them feel. This is valuable real estate they are not using. What an incredible waste. So, let's take a minute and be brutally honest with ourselves. Take a look at what's not working or what's depleting you when you look at your space.

Below are a few things the Great Designer loves to remove from our design. What else can you think of that needs to go?

"Whoever would foster love covers over an **offense**, but whoever repeats the matter separates close friends" (Proverbs 17:9).

"Get rid of all **bitterness**, **rage** and **anger**, **brawling** and **slander**, along with every form of **malice**. Be kind and compassionate to one another, forgiving each other, just as in Christ God forgave you" (Ephesians 4:31–32).

"Do not **judge**, and you will not be judged. Do not **condemn**, and you will not be condemned. Forgive, and you will be forgiven" (Luke 6:37).

"Instead of your **shame** you will receive a double portion, and instead of **disgrace** you will rejoice in your inheritance. And so you will inherit a double portion in your land, and everlasting joy will be yours" (Isaiah 61:7).

Notice how the **Great Designer** is always replacing that which is unredeemable with things of **great value** and **beauty**. He's amazing!

PART 2

DESIGN STEP 2

What needs to be REMOVED in your home and life to help create that vision, style, hope, or dream? What are the things you think a great designer would ask you to remove?

What makes you feel depleted in this home/room (e.g., color, style, lighting, etc.)?

What makes you feel depleted in your life (e.g., a relationship, a habit, a belief, etc.)?

What steals your peace and joy in this home/room (e.g., cleanliness, old ugly pieces, broken things, etc.)?

What steals your peace and joy in your life (e.g., unforgiveness, offense, generational curses, etc.)?

What causes you anxiety/worry in your home (e.g., clutter, dysfunction, furniture placement, etc.)?

What causes you anxiety/worry in your life (e.g., negative thoughts, fear, unbelief, etc.)?

CHAPTER NINE
REPURPOSE

BROKEN GIFTS AND MINDSETS

As a designer, I hate to see things wasted. Many people collect a multitude of things over the course of a lifetime. Some may seem frivolous or hold little value, but even those things can sometimes be repurposed for a completely different use in the grand scheme of the new design. So, don't be quick to throw out these things from your life or your home.

I remember as a young woman, when money was tight, a friend and I would drive up and down the streets of our small town on Fridays. That was trash day and we would load up furniture items that had been left out on the curb. It was a "cheap" thrill to drag them back home to sand, paint, and recreate them.

After we had filled our humble homes with these one-of-a-kind pieces, we couldn't stop. We saw possibilities in almost anything we came across, so the repurposing continued and we began to sell these treasures. It was a thrill to see them transformed, not to mention the great side hustle. This practice has not only come in handy with my current design business, but it has set me apart. I truly can recreate any space on little to no budget, if need be.

These one-of-a-kind items can add much character, warmth, and interest to any room. It's a ton of fun to create the perfect little piece for the ideal spot in your space at minimal to no cost! So, keep your eyes open for these types of items. They can easily be given new life with a little imagination, paint, and effort. Truly, the sky's your limit.

So how does this apply to our lives? We can see how God is in the business of repurposing things in our lives that can seem broken, dysfunctional, or insignificant, but how can we best partner with Him?

Much like we did in the removal process, we need to step back and take account of what we have. What is already ours? Should it be completely removed or is it redeemable, and if so, how can we repurpose it?

It is so freeing to know the God of the Universe is the one who wants to do this for us. The question is, why does He desire this? He has created us to have an intimate relationship with Him and He wants to construct a beautiful and majestic place for His Spirit to dwell. That place is our heart! Lucky us to have Him in charge of our renovation.

Think about it. Who are we that He patiently helps us remove the very things that put Him on the cross and broke His body and His heart?

In His holiness, He could easily have judged us and refused to be near us; instead, He partners with us on this journey of restoration. What an incredible privilege it is to know Him and be KNOWN by Him.

Oh, mighty Creator, have your way with us. As you rebuild us, may the same things that break your heart, break ours. Thank you for showing us what needs to be removed, and now we ask you to repurpose that which is redeemable in us and which will bring you the utmost honor and pleasure.

PART 2

Help us find what needs fixing.
Help us find our hidden treasures.
Help us have your vision for restoration.
In Jesus name, Amen

STEP 3

THE REPURPOSING OF BROKEN GIFTS AND MINDSETS

I was excited by the great strides the Designer had made in cleaning up my place, but I must confess I was deeply saddened by the realization of what my family had left for me. It was so oppressive and dark. How could this be? We were good people—they were good people, always striving to do what was expected of them.

As I was struggling with this ugly reality, the Designer came. He sat down next to me without saying a word. I wept and so did He. Strangely, He knew why I was sad. Without a word He brought comfort as He reassured me of His love. My mind searched for the answers. Who am I that this Great Designer cares for me?

At that moment, He took my hands and led me in a prayer to forgive them, those who came before me. He assured me that my forgiveness was very necessary for both them and for me. You see, this would break the generational curses that had been handed down with all the ugly pieces. My job was to bless and honor my ancestors who came before me. I was to ask the Father if there were any jobs given to them that were left unfinished. "If so Father, complete them through me," I cried!

I cried from a deep place I didn't know existed; something had shifted in me. After the tears stopped, He lifted my head and smiled, reminding me that not everything that had been passed down to me was unusable; in fact, there were hidden treasures to be uncovered. Something inside me came alive. New hope and vision had arrived.

This was all so exciting to think that He could use some of those old broken pieces. He reassured me if anything could be salvaged it would be His first priority. He would use every last worthy piece of my life. He was committed to repairing them all. What a life-giving thought that was to me. I could still use much of what was handed down to me from my family.

So as the Designer walked through my rooms again, looking for things that were usable, I held my breath in anticipation. What would He pull down from the shelves? To my amazement, He found value in things I took for granted and had overlooked for years.

The first thing was a beautiful, sturdy vase full of hard work and integrity, which had been handed down from my forefathers. I do remember my own father teaching me from this very special vase. The Designer said this was something we definitely needed to keep as it's an important piece that I will want to hand down to my children. But before I did, He would be cleaning it out a bit. He wanted to make sure He emptied it of any striving. Hmmm, I do remember that part, and it never felt good. I was so thankful for His willingness to remove it from that beautiful vase.

The next piece He pulled from the shelf would need a refinishing of sorts. It was my family's love for Him, my Designer. When I looked at it, tears welled up in my eyes. It was evidence they knew who He really was and desired to devote their lives to Him. But something had tarnished this gorgeous piece. He said it was the rules and regulations that had been forced on them; they tarnish everything. He would gladly buff it up, since I had also forgiven my family members. I cannot express how much this meant—that He was willing to do this for me and use it as a precious piece in my design.

He left the best for last. He brought out a basket full of broken pieces. What were these pieces? As I looked closer, again tears welled up in my eyes and ran down my cheeks. I had

PART 2

to pause to catch my breath. They were the deep heartaches I had walked through in life: my sister being handicapped, my dad dying at a young age, my insecurities as a teenager, my betrayal after twenty-six years of marriage, and all the other disappointments in between. They were ALL in that basket. I sobbed as I looked at them, all mixed in there together.

I personally watched Him as He put piece by piece of every broken part of my life back together again. I cannot explain how He did it, but I will testify on His behalf that He is an artist like no other. He used every broken piece to create something incredibly and indescribably beautiful. How could I ever repay Him for going over and above in repurposing all the brokenness in my heart?

He assured me these unique and precious items would be what He would use as inspiration for the entire design of my heart. How could things that were once so painful become so breathtakingly beautiful?

When He was done repurposing that which was broken, He began to find the perfect spot for each one. I was amazed by what I saw. It was as if they were all made for my life, my space. Each piece was perfect! So much love, so much life, so much goodness surrounded them all.

So, my friend, as you walk through this experience called Life by Design, be encouraged because NOTHING is wasted when you work with the Great Designer. He can create beauty from complete brokenness. Trust me—my entire life has been built from it and it's now a picture of **HOPE**.

"Not only so, but we also glory in our sufferings, because we know that suffering produces perseverance; perseverance, character; and character, hope. And **hope does not put us to shame**, because God's love has been poured out into our hearts through the Holy Spirit, who has been given to us" (Romans 5:3–5).

Please remember this: doing everything RIGHT—if you built it yourself—can still be WRONG. How can I say such a thing? Because without His design work and His ability to repurpose all our brokenness, it will never be all He has planned for us. So, I would encourage you to bring out all your broken pieces; don't hide even one. Allow Him to create something beautiful from them for He is able, He is trained, and He is highly creative as the Great Designer.

Repurposing is so important because the things we possess cannot only have great meaning to us, but they can be the very things that guide us to our destinies. They will show us how we were uniquely built for such a time as this. Everything we experience, whether good or bad, helps create this intricate story that is uniquely ours. It is a story we will use to touch our world and affect the eternal destiny of many others. This truly is the greatest story ever told.

So, let's partner with Him in this process.

I think if we are honest, we can all admit we have valuable things in our lives that are broken and in need of repair. Let's consider all our important relationships. Is there one, two, or more that need our attention? Some can be repaired by picking up the phone and having a much-needed heart-to-heart conversation, like a simple coat of paint. Others may need a counselor involved in the repair process, like taking our item to an expert to get it up and running again. Either way, we must not throw out that which has value merely because it doesn't look like it should or could at this moment in time.

Trust me, when we repair items such as these, they can change the entire design of our life. God wants us to take account of everything He has entrusted to us; He takes repurposing seriously. So, take the time to identify the broken things in your life and ask God how to take each one and bring it back to a place of honor or of good use.

Are there places or items in your life or home that are not functioning well? Are they obsolete, obstructing, or simply not working? In the design world, I find these to be the most challenging but also the most rewarding items to tackle. You see, as a designer, I'm a problem-solver first. When presented with design dilemmas, I must find a way to make things work by

PART 2

repurposing them into the design. Quite often, these "dilemmas" can become the focal point of the room, once the creative solution is found.

Let me share an example of a huge design dilemma I had years ago. We purchased an adorable house on the perfect little lot. The house was built in the 60's by a builder who was known for his cutting-edge designs and forward thinking. Many of the houses he built had an "interesting" feature. In our house, the kitchen had a beautiful brick wall, on the other side of which was a large fireplace. On the kitchen side of the brick wall was a large indoor grill, which no longer worked. It was bizarre to say the least and completely dysfunctional. Everyone who walked in said, "What is that?" in disgust. But I loved the brick and thought there must be something we could do. This was not our forever house so ripping down the whole brick wall along with the fireplace was not an option. But still, it looked like a large pizza oven housing a big black pit with a dirty old grill at the bottom of it. Eek!

What to do? I labored over this for weeks. Should I cover up the big grill or put something in it? Then the light bulb went on. I needed more counter space, and this was the era when coffee shops were the rage and bistro decor was huge. Oh my, this would be my coffee station. I could see it—filled with different flavored syrups along with a beautiful bowl containing different breakfast bars and biscottis. In my mind, I was already seeing all the possibilities and planning the details.

Now, the PROBLEM had become a source of excitement and wonderful possibilities. I quickly had a stainless-steel shelf made to fit perfectly inside, completely covering the ugly grill. Once it was installed, I realized I needed light in there. If I had light, I also needed electricity. Oh my! As we began to look at how it could be done, to our surprise we discovered an already existing outlet tucked up inside. We installed a beautiful light which created a wonderful ambient glow from above. This would become the coffee station of all coffee stations, for little to no money—simply a whole lot of imagination and stubborn determination.

Funny thing is, when it came time to sell the house it was actually one of the features the new homeowner loved the most. Why do I tell you this? Because I honestly believe there is a creative solution for every challenge or mess in our lives.

Such solutions arise from the ability to see or focus on the same circumstance or problem in a different way. Our Designer has an exceptional knack at doing exactly that in our lives. He is actually a show-off when it comes to this sort of thing, but I'm ok with it because He is so, so good at it. I just love Him!

There are many places in life where we can feel stuck and see only the problem. When things are not functioning, we tend to focus on that and not the infinite possibilities the situation is providing for us. This may be a stretch, but I don't think so. You see, it begins with our mindset and what we decide to focus on—the problem or the solution.

Let's start by first looking at what God wants us to focus on.

"Finally, brothers and sisters, whatever is **true**, whatever is **noble**, whatever is **right**, whatever is **pure**, whatever is **lovely**, whatever is **admirable**—if anything is **excellent** or praiseworthy—think about such things" (Philippians 4:8).

What would life look like if we thought about such things? What would happen if we focused on what was right rather than what was wrong? What if we became full of gratitude for what we did have? For example, what a gorgeous brick wall we have to work with. What an interesting and unique opening. What could this area provide for us? What do we need in this space? These types of questions can solve the biggest of problems.

Gratitude is a super power; it will literally change the way you see life, circumstances, and others. It opens your mind to what could be. This works every time in design.

Our problems can come in a variety of packages unique to us. Let's start with our spouse's "features." We can focus on what we don't like or we can flip it on its head in an act of gratitude.

PART 2

Here's a common frustration. Does your husband get home late from work too often? Is it irritating and frustrating? Does it affect the way you treat him when he comes in the door? What if you paused and asked yourself the question: what is good about this man?

You may say things like:

"Well, he is a hard worker."
"He is stable."
"He comes home every night."
"He spends long days providing for us."
"He works without being thanked."
"He is doing his best."
"He is the man I CHOOSE to love."

If you rehearsed these kinds of statements in your mind over and over, you would begin to see him in a whole new light. You would see more good things about him. Not only that, but he would feel the shift when he came home after a long day of work. How could something this simple solve a multitude of problems in your relationship? This will work in absolutely every area of your life.

Again, gratitude is a SUPER POWER; it can change EVERYTHING!

Whatever your circumstance or your problem looks like, I guarantee if you stop for a moment and write down all the things that are right and you continue to focus on these truths, your life will change in so many positive ways.

It is the most amazing thing I have done for my life. Do you know what gratitude produces? It produces JOY. When we begin to look through the eyes of gratitude, everything looks different. Before you start your day, thank God for 10 things.

If you're having a difficult time thinking of what you're truly grateful for, do this: imagine if you were only left with the things you thanked God for today. Would your list now include things like health, family, finances, and freedom? These are things we often take for granted.

If you desire to get unstuck or move away from a life that is focusing on the wrong things, start with the way you think—your mindset. Start with gratitude to repurpose a mind that sees what's wrong and develop a mind that sees what is right. This one truth will radically change the **interior** of your life.

"Do not be anxious about anything, but in every situation, by prayer and petition, with **thanksgiving**, present your requests to God. And the **peace** of God, which transcends all understanding, will **guard your hearts** and **your minds** in Christ Jesus" (Philippians 4:6–7).

PART 2

DESIGN STEP 3

What needs to be REPURPOSED and is salvageable, worthy of new life and repair?
What is broken in your home?
What is broken in your life?
What is needed to repair this area in your home?
What is needed to repair this area in your life?
What is not functioning well in your home and how can you refocus with gratitude?
What is not functioning well in your life and how can you refocus with gratitude?

CHAPTER TEN
REDEEM

THE BLUEPRINT TO OUR DESTINY

As a designer I have an ultimate design plan in mind, a blueprint of sorts. This is after understanding my client's likes, dislikes, personality, style, needs, and budget. I then come up with a step-by-step plan. However, the process unfolds one choice at a time. With each decision my client makes, the plan either moves forward or has to be adjusted. The more they trust me the better the plan is executed and completed in a timely manner.

Isn't this a sobering thought when we contemplate the design of our lives? How often do we hamper or slow down the design of our lives? Maybe we've never been introduced to the Great Designer. Maybe we don't know Him well enough to trust Him with such a massive job. Maybe we think we have it all under control. We are all in a different place and that's okay.

I can only speak for myself. He has been there actively in my past, planning, preparing and guiding me through the uncertainty, the heartache, and the joyous moments. All to arrive here in my present, where He is again preparing me for my future and all it holds. This is *Kairos Time*, friends!

It's all so wonderful and complex while still being simple. It begins to come together as we allow Him to guide us through this glorious life-transforming process, one step at a time. Remember all that He creates is beautiful, but He must be given complete control of the design. This is the **key**.

When I started this journey with Him, I thought I had a pretty good idea of what my place would look like in the end. The work has been much more extensive than I could have imagined. At times, I thought the demo process would never end. Often, I wanted to move, run away, or start over somewhere . . . anywhere. But His reassuring voice has kept me doing the work, pursuing the end results only He can see. I cannot explain how miraculous and detailed His work is; it simply must be experienced for oneself.

STEP 4

REDEMPTION IS THE BLUEPRINT TO OUR DESTINY

I decided to get to the dwelling early so I could stroll around a bit. Honestly, I barely recognize the place anymore. It's hard to believe all the work that's been done, all the things that we have accomplished. There have been so many changes I thought would be impossible. But step-by-step, He continued to give me detailed instructions exactly when I needed them. I shake my head in amazement when I look at some of the "before" pictures and compare them to where I am now in the process.

I'm shocked at the difference it made to haul away all the junk. It really gave us a better view of what needed to be done next. That was such an important step. Oh, and I can't wait for people to see how He has repurposed all my unique pieces. He actually never stops working on them. He is constantly refining them and it's evident the details are very important to Him.

I shudder to think of all the valuable things I may have seen as useless and thrown out if He hadn't been there to share His vision with me and how these things could be used in my design. In fact, they are the very pieces that have been so critical in rebuilding the framework of my life, which He has now placed on a firm foundation. I must say, this place is really coming together.

If I ever doubted His abilities, I certainly don't anymore! He has been showing me glimpses of what He has planned for some of the spaces. I kid you not, this is going to have the WOW factor one day. He's coming to show me some of the new pieces He will be bringing in soon. He told me they would complement all my current belongings.

This is the mark of a true designer—someone who can take what you already possess, improve upon it, then add new pieces to create a seamless masterpiece. It's as if it was all destined to be used together.

When He arrived, I shared with Him how I had been admiring the place and how thankful I was for the incredible job He has done so far. He smiled at me and rolled out the blueprints. I was beyond excited to finally see them. Even though they weren't complete, I could see where He was going with things.

He said, "Your foundations have been made firm. We have moved out a considerable amount of trash and we are now working with a solid framework." He seemed pleased with the work we had done thus far. He began to go over the different rooms in my house. He assured me as we worked on each one, my home's true identity would be revealed. Things were getting interesting and I couldn't wait for Him to go over all the unique rooms in my house.

This is where the awkward part came in. He leaned forward and said, "There seem to be a couple of rooms I haven't been able to get access to yet and I would like to take a look at them."

PART 2

You could've heard a pin drop. I was horrified and stunned by His request. I didn't think the conversation would go there, not today anyway. I actually hadn't given those rooms much thought lately, with all the other work that had been going on. It overwhelmed me to think about the other rooms. Besides, I didn't even know where to start. I guess that's why I locked them up so many years ago.

He assured me we would use the same process and go piece by piece as we figured out together what stays and what goes. So, I took a deep breath and said, "Okay, if you'll help me, I will give you the keys." With a sigh of relief, He took the keys and said, "Thank you, I have great plans for these spaces too." Spoken like the true Designer He is.

In fact, He never seems to tire of helping me clean up the mess. Ever since I've given Him access, he's been working pretty much non-stop to redeem those forgotten areas of my heart too. He is relentless in His pursuit of uncovering the truth of who I am.

It definitely feels better to have all the doors unlocked and open. There is a tremendous amount of light flowing through them now. The only difficult thing is, I don't have many places left where I can hide my insecurities. They are really ugly, so I'm not crazy about them being left out in the open for anyone walking by to see.

The Designer said He'd be glad to take them away for me. Besides, He won't have any need for them in His master plan. Oh, how I desire to give them all to Him. I'm hoping someday soon I will be able to part with each and every one of them. The other rooms are becoming nothing short of beautiful, even though they are still a work in progress.

Well, maybe I should give you a quick tour of the place now, since it's all coming together. Get ready for something different. My Designer says He has done an infinite number of these designs and each is unique. How mind-boggling is that? However, there is one element that is the same in all of them. I'll take you there first.

I'm not sure how to describe this space, but I will try. It is the very center of my dwelling. You see, it's the most ornate room of them all. I love how it is circular, with no corners and no ceiling. It's my Designer's trademark; He calls it an "open heaven." Look up—isn't it breathtaking? It's lit by all the stars and is the biggest room of all. If you notice, this room has doors that lead directly to every other room in the house. You can access each one of them from this room. How incredible is that?

Even though this room is huge, you'll notice it only has one chair in it; well actually, it's called a throne.

This is what we call the THRONE ROOM. Look at it. Have you ever seen anything like it? I can't stop staring at it; it's so intricately detailed. I haven't told you the best part yet. I asked the Designer, along with His Son and the Holy Spirit, to come and live in the dwelling with me. Where they go one, they go all; they're literally inseparable. The Father will take His rightful place on the throne. You'll notice that I left plenty of room around it so I can kneel before Him and worship. I love how the Holy Spirit is always helping me. His sweet presence changes the atmosphere in this place.

The Designer, well, He actually paid for the place. Unbelievable, right? As soon as I invited them in and told them the place was theirs to do whatever they wanted, the Designer announced that He'd bought it—it's been paid for in full. I no longer have to pay for anything that has been done to it. It's still hard to comprehend a gift of this magnitude.

Oh, and by the way, the angels play here day and night. They never stop singing, *"Holy, Holy, Holy!"* It's definitely their favorite song and mine too, now. I thought I may tire of it, but when I'm in His presence there are no other words that come to me. I am in AWE.

Let me show you the smallest, most intimate room in my dwelling. It's where we meet privately and is where much is accomplished. We call it the SECRET PLACE. Our deepest conversations happen here. The Designer is often helping me make my request known to the Father here. He always knows exactly what to ask for when I'm not even sure and words escape me.

This is the safest place in the Universe. I have made my way in here countless times when the world was far too much for me and the pain was too great. He allows me to hide under the feathers of His wings where I stay until the fear and worry pass in the dark of night. He has never once turned me away, not once.

The Holy Spirit provides all the comfort needed here. Oh, how I love this room. This is where I sing to Him as I present my gifts of gratitude to Him. With each breath, I worship Him and I become lost in His goodness and love.

My innermost thoughts are shared with Him and nothing is hidden or rejected. I am fully embraced by the One who formed me. I was created for this place. I probably shouldn't have started by showing you these rooms because, if you're like me, you won't want to leave. But we should move on now.

We've spent a considerable amount of time on the rooms that hold my gifts and talents. I love spending time in my CREATIVE ROOM. It was definitely built solely for me. It's the room that holds all my "out of the box" ideas and creations.

I think it's my favorite place to hang out and just DREAM BIG. My Designer laughs at me and says, "Are you in here again? Come on, let's focus on a few other rooms we need to get busy on. You can come back here as soon as we are done."

He teases me and says I see a lot of "shiny things." That makes me laugh. I think He likes that part of me. In fact, I know He does or He wouldn't have made me like this. My creative room is the size of a gymnasium. I'm not sure what I'm going to do with all the space yet but He said He wanted me to have plenty of room for growth. Wow, I really appreciate that.

Okay, ready? This next room is the room I love. I am in and out of here constantly. It's my CONNECTION ROOM. I think my Designer named it after me. He reminds me often that I am His "little connector." So, He designed a room specifically for that. Do you see all the comfy chairs set up close to each other?

This is where we share our hearts with one another. There are chairs here of every style. I personally love the vintage-looking ones that are covered in a rich-looking velvet.

The people I meet here are so different that my Designer wanted all of them to have a specific chair in which they would feel comfortable. He thinks of every last detail. We have restaurant tables set up along one side so we can talk while having a meal. On the other side of the room is the most wonderful spot to have parties. There's nothing better than to invite all my friends whom I meet with one-on-one and then introduce them to each other. It's incredible to watch them connect with one another.

The Designer is always invited to these gatherings; He is the life of the party. They all adore Him; He literally lights up the room. Those guests who have not yet met Him personally, always stay around longer in hopes of learning more about Him and what makes Him so attractive. I love throwing parties in honor of Him. It's so easy; I simply invite people and He takes it from there. You see, He has a way of capturing their hearts as He speaks life over them. It's never a party without Him.

Let's move on. The next is the ENCOURAGER'S ROOM. It's painted with a beautiful color called *compassion*. Have you ever seen such a beautiful shade? It's soft and soothing and very unpretentious. This room is dear to me. Don't mind the carpet; it's pretty stained from all the tears that have been shed here. Both the Designer and I thought it best not to replace it. Somehow, it adds a depth to the decor, as it's a wonderful reminder of all the healing that has taken place in this room.

You see, encouragement is a powerful thing to give out whenever you can. It can change the course of a life. It changed mine when I was so desperately sad and felt completely lost in this world. Each encouraging word was like a life-raft that kept me afloat one more day in a raging, angry sea.

I will never forget those who were sent to encourage me and have compassion on me. I believe the Designer wants us all to have a similar room. It may be decorated quite differently

PART 2

depending on what we have experienced in this life and how we have been healed. This room will reflect and attract others who feel comfortable with this type of decor. The amazing thing about this room is, the more you use it to help others, the bigger it grows in your own house.

Here's another door; let's take a peek. It's my COMMUNICATION ROOM. Funny, right? I have always been a communicator. Communication started early on in my life, even though it was a bit misguided. I had many report cards sent home with the comment section on the back reading something like this: *"Is friendly, courteous, and overall, a good student, but she talks too much."* Or, *"We've had to move her seat three times this grading period due to outbursts of laughter."* Or, *"Doesn't work well alone."*

For some strange reason, I always felt the need to make a comment, a face, or a joke. I honestly thought those were my only options.

I loved having friends, laughing, and communicating in any way I could—and I still do. I'm an extrovert and I come alive when connecting with others. That's probably why my Designer put my Connection Room right next to my Communications Room.

Isn't it amazing how He ties it all together? I can carry items back and forth between all these different rooms and they work in each space. The colors and style flow perfectly throughout my dwelling from each specific room. The Designer says these rooms make up my true IDENTITY.

He orchestrates our identities in such a fascinating and incredible way. My heart is for you to know who He has created you to be and for what purpose. This is *your* IDENTITY. When we grasp who has designed us and for what, it changes everything.

Let's look at your **gifts**, your **talents**, and your **interests**. How do they help create your rooms? How do all these areas work together for God to be able to use your life while also creating a beautiful place for Him in the throne room of your heart?

In my job of design, I meet people every day whom I would not meet otherwise. When I delve into creating something beautiful for them, they light up and they also open up to me. This is when I can share something much greater than beautiful colors and beautiful design. I can share my heart and the heart of God. So, whatever it is that He has placed in you—whether it be a love for gardening, or cooking, or business—ask how can you use it for Him? This is a powerful question that will lead you to your **purpose**.

He will use our strengths and talents in new and innovative ways as they work together to expand our reach in this world. For instance, the writing of this book is far from my comfort zone, in fact, it couldn't be farther. It has been a labor of love as I share my deepest struggles with you and give you a glimpse into my redesign in hopes you will find the courage to go deeper and trust Him more and more with your own design.

He loves to STRETCH us. Don't get me wrong, I have always been a communicator of sorts; remember I like to talk . . . but writing? I would normally avoid it at all costs. So, what did He ask of me?

You got it. He asked me to share with you AND put it in writing. Can you hear the STRETCHING that's going on over here? I'm a very animated communicator so, for me, texting is much easier because of the hundreds of emojis I can pepper throughout my writing. I'm pushing through the discomfort for you . . . for Him. Hopefully, you can imagine an emoji or two, or let's say a thousand throughout my writing.

Now, let's dig a little deeper and focus on the pieces we feel to be insignificant: our personal interests, our quirks, our likes, and dislikes. As believers, we often think these types of things are silly or of no eternal use. That, however, couldn't be farther from the truth. God designs us with all of these wonderful differences and He is excited to see us stepping out and using them all. These are the miraculous ways He moves through us.

Let's take a look at what He has placed within you for your great design. Oh, friend, be confident in who He made **you**.

"For you created my inmost being; you knit me together in my mother's womb. I praise you because I am **fearfully** and **wonderfully made**; your works are **wonderful**, I know that full well" (Psalm 139:13–14).

"The word of the Lord came to me, saying, 'Before I formed you in the womb **I knew you**, before you were born **I set you apart**; I appointed you as a **prophet to the nations**'" (Jeremiah 1:4–5).

"And we know that in all things God works for the good of those who love him, who have been called according to his **purpose**" (Romans 8:28).

"The people I formed for myself that they may **proclaim my praise**" (Isaiah 43:21).

He is so worthy of our **praise**. His plans for us are **great**. We have been set apart for His **purposes**.

DESIGN STEP 4

What SPECIAL ITEMS do you possess that would work well in the new design of your home?
What GIFTINGS and TALENTS do you possess that are working well in your life?
Describe your emerging STYLE; what does it look like? Tell me what you like most about it.
Describe your emerging IDENTITY; what does it look like? Tell me what you like most about it.
What is UNIQUE about your home or the decorative pieces you possess? How could they be used creatively?
What is UNIQUE about your personality and the qualities you possess? How could they be used creatively?

CHAPTER ELEVEN
REALIZE

YOUR PURPOSE

After the proper steps are taken and decisions are made, it becomes clear what the style and purpose of each room will be. The homeowner is left with not only beautiful spaces, but functional spaces—spaces that not only provide peace and comfort to the family, but entertain and accommodate others as well.

It is at this point where we begin to focus on the details. DESIGN really is all in the DETAILS—it's the small things, the small moments, the small gestures that create a beautiful design. This is true not only in our home, but in our lives.

As the design comes closer to completion, the rooms of our identity also take shape. It becomes easier to answer these age-old questions, which I believe to be necessary to move on to our final design step called Realization.

Why am I here?
Who am I?

What is my purpose?

After going through this process myself, He has been revealing these very answers to me. Let me share with you what He has shown me through my own personal journey. I hope it will be a road map to help you find your own answers.

1) Why am I here?
    I understand I was created by Him and for Him. I am known by Him in every way. He has proven His love for me in the past and in the present, and because of that, I am confident He will do the same in the future. He knows how fragile and broken I am because He understands the state of mankind. Regardless, He still desires to have not only a connection with me, but a deep love relationship with me, His creation.

2) Who am I?
    He has shown me who I am; He has never once judged me for who I am not. It has never been about what I should be, but rather a discovery of who I was created to be. That truth may be difficult to wrap your mind around, but this process has revealed it to me in a way I have never been able to completely grasp before. He liked me even before He cleaned me up and fixed me and gave me new life and hope. I am His child and He sees me as worthy of love.

3) What is my purpose?
    When I discovered why I was here and who I was created to be, my destiny and purpose began to unfold as I learned I am a unique composite of my Father. You see, His beauty is so vast, I am but a glimmer of His many facets fashioned in a specific way to fulfill a particular purpose on this earth, which is to bring glory to Him! I am to be His hands and feet on this earth.

PART 2

STEP 5

THE REALIZATION OF YOUR PURPOSE

Last time I met with the Designer, He had given me an overview of the work that had been done; He called them my blueprints. Now I had a good idea of how the whole structure was going to look, but not everything had been revealed to me yet. He left with me some strong desires and ideas to contemplate. However, it was still unclear how all the rooms of my identity would function together for His ultimate plan.

He was about to reveal more of His plan to me and the suspense was almost too much. There were days I dreamt about what it would look like; other times, I wanted to start doing the work myself already. I was becoming concerned that maybe He had forgotten the importance of the work that was yet to be done.

Silly me, I should have known better that starting without Him would be a mistake, and even slow down the process.

But like always, He showed up right on time. He came in with the plans in hand; these were much more detailed than before. He said, "Before I show you everything, I want you to take a walk with me."

He led me to the THRONE ROOM, where we had a wonderful conversation about all He had done in my dwelling and how He was beyond excited about my future with Him. He told me He had been preparing a special room for me and that it had much to do with the purpose for my life.

Needless to say, He had my full attention. He took me by the hand and there before me I saw two doors, different from all the rest. They were ancient-looking iron doors and as they opened everything shifted, including my perception of the Designer.

He looked like a King, full of glory and ready for battle. My mind raced for answers; what was I seeing and what was this place? The once kind and patient Designer was now a fierce and mighty warrior. He turned to me and said, "I have been preparing you for such a time as this."

My eyes widened and my knees weakened in His presence. I wanted to drop to the floor because I was completely undone. The sound of His powerful voice shook the room and the authority He possessed was incomprehensible. He held me up and looked me in the eyes and said, "This is where we will operate from."

In my confusion I said, "What is this place? What have you prepared for me?"

He said, "It is your WAR ROOM and I have placed in you everything you will need to carry out the mission I have for you on this earth. Every gift, every desire, and every experience will be used to empower, encourage and connect you to other warriors. You have a unique crown that will be worn because of the creativity I have placed within you, before the beginning of time. You and the others shall be a crown of beauty in the hand of the Lord, and a royal diadem in the hand of your God. We will meet in the SECRET PLACE daily. It is there where you will get your orders as you gain wisdom and strength from me. Do not fear my child, for I will go before you and I will go behind you and I will go around you. I will also send an Army of Warring Angels to fight with you and protect you and the others."

For a split second, my knees shook beneath me. "What? Little, old me? You want to send me?"

Then He rolled out the plan and my heart pounded with excitement as I saw my assignment. Tears welled up in my eyes and a lump formed in my throat. I couldn't believe how perfect His plan was; every last part of me was built for it. My mind, body, and soul cried, "YES, send me!" He was absolutely right. All His selfless and loving hard work had prepared me for this moment in history. I had found my purpose in this life and my place in advancing His Kingdom.

Oh, my goodness, you guys; that's my assignment: to communicate truth and wisdom from His heart to yours in my quirky and creative way! I'm to connect and encourage women to allow Him to design their dwellings to be a worthy place for Him to reside, so you too can find your identity within the dwelling and find your purpose in the secret place. ONLY He can pull that off.

Looking back now I can see how He was training me my entire life for this mission. Even before I called Him for the consultation and knew I needed His help, He was planning, and preparing, and lining up everything I would need.

While going through the process, I had caught a glimpse of His long and detailed list. My whole life was on it. He reassured me nothing is wasted when He's in charge of a building project. Some of the materials were . . . well, let's say unexpected. Did you know He uses suffering quite a bit in His building projects? He said when it's used correctly, it gives the structure extraordinary strength, like nothing else can.

That's why He doesn't always remove suffering, but rather teaches us how to move through it while guiding us by the hand, and even carrying us if needed. During these difficult times, we learn the mysteries of who He is and who we are in Him. The journey can be deep and dark, but He has been faithful to give us His word which is a lamp unto our feet and light unto our path. It is on the path of suffering that great deposits of perseverance, character, and hope are made.

"Not only so, but we also glory in our sufferings, because we know that suffering produces **perseverance**; perseverance, character; and **character, hope**" (Romans 5:3–4).

"I consider that our present sufferings are not worth comparing with the **glory** that will be revealed in us" (Romans 8:18).

Oh, how the human heart dreads the thought of suffering, we spend our lives trying to avoid it at all cost; comfort is all we seek. We forget Jesus chose the path of suffering to save our very lives. It's in that truth we will find true comfort. May we learn to walk in confidence knowing that the one who sacrificed everything for us will walk with us on our path of suffering.

"To this you were called, because Christ suffered **for you**, leaving you an example, that you should follow in his steps" (1 Peter 2:21).

"For just as we share abundantly in the sufferings of Christ, so also our **comfort** abounds through Christ" (2 Corinthians 1:5).

"And the God of **all grace**, who called you to his eternal glory in Christ, after you have suffered a little while, will himself **restore** you and make you **strong**, **firm** and **steadfast**" (1 Peter 5:10).

Let me tell you something I have learned in this highly imperfect life of mine. Are you ready? **Nothing** is wasted! No experience, no heartache—big or small—is wasted when the creator is at work in our lives. He uses it all to create a story that is uniquely ours and a destiny so great we cannot fathom what He has planned for us.

My prayer is that you would understand He has been there all along and He is not mad at you. I challenge you to shift your thinking, stop living in regret, shame, or wishing things were different.

Your story is *yours*; no one has one like it and He wants to help you tell it. Through this process you will experience healing and through that healing you will have compassion for others who have walked a similar path. As you bring comfort to them, more healing will come to you. His ways are so much higher than ours.

"Praise be to the God and Father of our Lord Jesus Christ, the Father of **compassion** and the God of all **comfort**" (2 Corinthians 1:3).

"Carry each other's burdens, and in this way you will fulfill the law of Christ" (Galatians 6:2).

The ability to hear His VOICE is key for any true success in Kingdom work. Over the years, I've been a self-help junky. How to be a successful mom, how to be a successful business person, how to be a successful Christian, and so on. After reading countless books I found one common thread in them

PART 2

all: to take control of your morning and plan your day without interruption and without distraction.

"But seek first his kingdom and his righteousness, and all these things will be given to you as well" (Matthew 6:33).

First fruits of the morning must be HIS. Put the cell phone away—like in another room. Don't check emails, notifications, or news. Sounds crazy but it's not. If you want to hear His voice and have intimacy with Him, you must close out the world and take control of your mind. We must take our mind captive to make it obedient to Christ. This is no easy task when we are inundated with Instagram, Facebook, and today's news. It is an overwhelming avalanche of information that causes great confusion, massive distraction, and in the midst of which, it's impossible to take our minds captive. It must be completely silenced.

"We demolish arguments and every pretension that sets itself up against the knowledge of God, and we take **captive every thought** to make it obedient to Christ" (2 Corinthians 10:5).

The morning is a powerful time when the mind can receive information at its highest level; it is clear, rested, and ready to learn. Take this valuable time to quiet yourself. If it helps, put on soft, instrumental worship music and find a comfortable place to sit, void of clutter.

You may want to start by journaling, which is nothing more than writing your prayers out. This practice has been very helpful for me over the years to keep my mind focused as I tend to be easily distracted. I literally write whatever is on my mind; sometimes it's barely legible but that doesn't matter as it's only for my eyes and His. I share with Him what's on my heart, and what my concerns are. I ask Him questions and then this is the best part: I **wait** for Him to answer me and then I write down what He impresses on my heart.

These journals are priceless to go back over and read; they have been life-changing for me. They are a beautiful reminder of prayers answered and words spoken to me from a Holy

God. When I begin to write what I hear Him saying, I mark it with a star, so I often grab an old journal and page through it, reading the starred sections. These are like gold and precious stones to me. They come alive off the page and give me much needed directions at the perfect time.

Then I read His word, His beautiful word. I am in awe that I know this mighty God who conquers the armies of men and who performs great miracles. This is the same God who speaks to me and waits to speak to you. I'm telling you, there are mornings I can barely wait to get up and sit with Him and hear from Him. I encourage you to take whatever steps you need to create such a place to meet with Him.

Pray and journal; share your heart with Him and then quiet yourself and ask Him to speak to you. Stay in the silence as long as it takes and you will develop the ability to hear His soft, sweet, and powerful voice.

You will be surprised by the insight and wisdom He will give you. This practice is vital for the direction you will need as you partner with Him to find your destiny and then fulfill it. This has been a complete game-changer for me.

See what the Bible says about this important practice.

"Keep this Book of the Law always on your lips; **meditate** on it day and night, so that you may be careful to do everything written in it. Then you will be **prosperous** and **successful**. Have I not commanded you? Be **strong** and **courageous**. Do not be afraid; do not be discouraged, for the Lord your God will be with you wherever you go" (Joshua 1:8–9).

I hope you have enjoyed gaining a peek into my own personal transformation and have gotten a few ideas for your own. Everyone's design and mission will look a bit different because of your unique story, but before we part, I would like to highlight the rooms that are absolutely vital in everyone's design.

We will start with the THRONE ROOM. We must all decide who we will allow to sit on the throne of our hearts. Trust me when I say if He is invited to take His rightful place

PART 2

there, He will be faithful in helping you build your life and align your destiny to accomplish what you have been placed here to do. This room was created for Him and **Him alone**. When His presence is not there, regardless of how much cleaning, rearranging, and renovating we do, it will amount to nothing more than an abandoned pile of rubble that serves no purpose for eternity.

"Therefore, if anyone is in Christ, the **new creation** has come: The old has gone, **the new is here**" (2 Corinthians 5:17).

"So then, just as you received Christ Jesus as Lord, continue to live your lives in him, rooted and built up in him, **strengthened** in the **faith** as you were taught, and **overflowing** with **thankfulness**" (Colossians 2:6–7).

Make plans to meet with Him in the SECRET PLACE we spoke of above; it is Holy ground. He waits for you; He longs for you to sit with Him and learn of Him. It is in the quietness that you will hear His voice and plans will be revealed. We must first learn to pull away from all that distracts us. We must guard this time as if our lives depended on it because they do. Our destinies, our children's destinies, and the destinies of those we were born to touch with our stories, **depend on it.**

The enemy is shrewd in the way he consumes our attention through these great distractions of life. Media, social media, and even our goals—none of which are necessarily bad—can pull us out of the process unless we are making time for Him first. This is the KEY.

Jesus knew this to be true. Prior to every great kingdom event demonstrated by Jesus, the Bible indicates that He got alone with God and spent time in prayer. During those quiet times, Jesus was establishing God's divine agenda in the earthly realm and downloading victory, success, and prosperity into His day while dislodging evil. He was taking control of the morning and taking authority over His day.

"Very early in the morning, while it was still dark, Jesus got up, left the house and went off to a **solitary place**, where he **prayed**" (Mark 1:35).

"After he had dismissed them, he went up on a mountainside **by himself** to pray. Later that night, he was there **alone**" (Matthew 14:23).

Jesus would often find a quiet place and get alone. He prayed before, after, and during important events and decisions. He knew the importance of the secret place and spent much of His time there. Let's follow His lead as we make big and small decisions for our lives.

Immediately before choosing His twelve apostles, He prayed: "One of those days Jesus went out to a mountainside to **pray**, and **spent the night praying** to God" (Luke 6:12).

Before teaching His disciples how to pray: "One day Jesus was praying in a certain place. When he finished, one of his disciples said to him, "**Lord, teach us to pray**, just as John taught his disciples" (Luke 11:1).

After the multiplication of loaves: "After leaving them, he went up on a mountainside to pray" (Mark 6:46).

Before the crucifixion, in the Garden of Gethsemane: "Then Jesus went with his disciples to a place called Gethsemane, and he said to them, 'Sit here while I go over there and pray.' He took Peter and the two sons of Zebedee along with him, and he began to be sorrowful and troubled. Then he said to them, 'My soul is overwhelmed with sorrow to the point of death. Stay here and keep watch with me.' Going a little farther, he fell with his face to the ground and prayed, 'My Father, if it is possible, may this cup be taken from me. Yet not as I will, but as you will.' Then he returned to his disciples and found them sleeping. 'Couldn't you men keep watch with me for one hour?' he asked Peter. 'Watch and pray so that you will not fall into temptation. The spirit is willing, but the flesh is weak.' He went away a second time and prayed, 'My Father, if it is not possible for this cup to be taken away unless I drink it, may your will be done.' When he came back, he again found them sleeping, because their eyes were heavy. So he left them and went away once more and prayed the third time, saying the same thing. Then he returned to the disciples and said to them, 'Are you

PART 2

still sleeping and resting? Look, the hour has come, and the Son of Man is delivered into the hands of sinners" (Matthew 26:36–45; also see Mark 14:32–41 and Luke 22:39–46).

If we are to carry out our mission, we need a WAR ROOM. After we have spent time in the SECRET PLACE with Him, we will begin to make plans according to the instructions we have received. We train hard with the weapons provided for us in His word.

"Finally, be strong in the Lord and in his mighty power. Put on the full armor of God, so that you can take your stand against the devil's schemes. For our struggle is not against flesh and blood, but against the rulers, against the authorities, against the powers of this dark world and against the spiritual forces of evil in the heavenly realms. Therefore put on the full armor of God, so that when the day of evil comes, you may be able to stand your ground, and after you have done everything, to stand. Stand firm then, with the belt of truth buckled around your waist, with the breastplate of righteousness in place, and with your feet fitted with the readiness that comes from the gospel of peace. In addition to all this, take up the shield of faith, with which you can extinguish all the flaming arrows of the evil one. Take the helmet of salvation and the sword of the Spirit, which is the word of God. And pray in the Spirit on all occasions with all kinds of prayers and requests. With this in mind, be alert and always keep on praying for all the Lord's people" (Ephesians 6:10–18).

Here in the WAR ROOM, we should study to show ourselves approved and hone our unique skills for the battle. Plans to advance His kingdom are made here as He intricately connects us with other warriors who will join us to complete His mission.

Every room He has placed in our identity is connected to this WAR ROOM and will need to be accessed to carry out our specific assignments. Embrace who He has designed you to be. Become familiar with what He has placed in each of your rooms.

Great power comes from being authentic and vulnerable as you minister and operate in your gifts. This may not sound like a war tactic, but I assure you it is. The enemy seeks to fracture our foundations and fill our rooms with insecurities in an attempt to hide our true identity and our purpose in this life. This is because he is well aware of the danger we present to his dark and hideous kingdom when we understand who we really are.

"You will be a crown of splendor in the LORD's hand, a royal diadem in the hand of your God" (Isaiah 62:3).

We are His *Restoration Royals*, an army of mighty warriors who know WHO they are and WHOSE they are!

The REALIZATION of this fact is what the enemy has tried to steal from us our entire existence. He has failed. Let us advance in every arena in which God has strategically placed us, knowing full well we have been placed here for such a time as this. I'm so stoked to battle with you all.

The amazing thing is, as I review my past it is changing my present. This is a profound truth that I have discovered through this process. God spoke to me when I began to write my section of this book, and this is what He said: "THIS WILL BE WRITTEN IN REAL TIME." I was quiet for a moment and thought, "What does that mean?" And then I heard it again. "THIS WILL BE WRITTEN IN REAL TIME!" I really wasn't sure what He meant by that then, but now I do.

During the writing of this book, there were many times I had to remove myself from all distractions. I had to quiet myself and reflect on my experiences in this life and how they brought me to this place. As I did, He began to give me new revelations on things that had taken place in my past. Through that, I received some inner healing along with new truth and wisdom for my present situations. I and my perspective were changing as I wrote (in real time).

This information is now preparing me for what He has planned in my future. This is similar to how God uses prophecy in His word: it gives us a glimpse of His faithfulness in the past, which imparts wisdom and courage for today, which then alters and directs our future. Our past, present, and future flow and intertwine together like some kind of a majestic painting created by God's perfect timing—*KAIROS TIME*!

Let's recap the necessary design steps:

RECOGNIZE the need for a Designer.
REMOVE the unredeemable collection.
REPURPOSE broken gifts and mindsets.
REDEEM the blueprints to your destiny.
REALIZE your purpose through God's Royal Design.

KEYS FOR DESIGNING A BEAUTIFUL LIFE

Suffering is useful

As you go into battle, you will need to understand suffering is useful. Your suffering is never in vain. What the enemy sought to destroy your life with, you will use against him. That very thing will become a mighty weapon in your arsenal, and it will be used to encourage and save others from his dastardly plans.

In fact, scripture says He "comforts us in all our troubles, so that we can comfort those in any trouble with the comfort we ourselves receive from God" (2 Corinthians 1:4).

Boom, that's how it works! (Insert dancing emoji.)

Get alone to hear God's voice

Your time alone with God will be absolutely essential as you seek to hear His voice for direction. Limiting the distractions of this world and putting Him first in the day will give you the edge you need to be successful on your mission.

"God's voice thunders in marvelous ways; he does great things beyond our understanding" (Job 37:5).

"When he has brought out all his own, he goes on ahead of them, and his sheep follow him because they know his voice" (John 10:4).

And sometimes He whispers to us. "After the earthquake came a fire, but the LORD was not in the fire. And after the fire came a gentle whisper" (1 Kings 19:12).

God's Word transforms your mind

The most precious commodity in the earthly realm is the mind. Not only is God vying for your minds, but the enemy is vying for your minds as well. In the last days, the intellectual property of the soul will be one of the commodities bought and sold in the marketplace and used to drive entire economies.

"The merchants of the earth will weep and mourn over her because no one buys their cargoes anymore—cargoes of gold, silver, precious stones and pearls; fine linen, purple, silk and scarlet cloth; every sort of citron wood, and articles of every kind made of ivory, costly wood, bronze, iron and marble; cargoes of cinnamon and spice, of incense, myrrh and frankincense, of wine and olive oil, of fine flour and wheat; cattle and sheep; horses and carriages; and human beings sold as slaves. They will say, 'The fruit you longed for is gone from you. All your luxury and splendor have vanished, never to be recovered.' The merchants who sold these things and gained their wealth from her will stand far off, terrified at her torment. They will weep and mourn and cry out: 'Woe! Woe to you, great city, dressed in fine linen, purple and scarlet, and glittering with gold, precious stones and pearls'" (Revelation 18:11–16).

So, you must saturate your mind with the Word of God so He can impart wisdom, courage, and strength to you, while transforming your mind into that of a warrior.

"For the word of God is alive and active. Sharper than any double-edged sword, it penetrates even to dividing soul and spirit, joints and marrow; it judges the thoughts and attitudes of the heart" (Hebrews 4:12).

Being empowered with the Holy Spirit

We must repent, be baptized, and receive the Holy Spirit. The Holy Spirit will guide you and comfort you every step of the way while giving you great power and authority to do what you have been called to do.

"Peter replied, 'Repent and be baptized, every one of you, in the name of Jesus Christ for the forgiveness of your sins. And you will receive the gift of the Holy Spirit'" (Acts 2:38).

The Holy Spirit empowers us to do many miraculous things for our good and His glory. By the power of the Holy Spirit, we can boldly proclaim the gospel.

"But you will receive power when the Holy Spirit comes on you; and you will be my witnesses in Jerusalem, and in all Judea and Samaria, and to the ends of the earth" (Acts 1:8).

The Holy Spirit can **help us pray** when we don't know how.

"In the same way, the Spirit helps us in our weakness. We do not know what we ought to pray for, but the Spirit himself intercedes for us through wordless groans" (Romans 8:26).

In Him we can abound in hope and be **filled** with **joy** and **peace**.

"May the God of hope fill you with all joy and peace as you trust in him, so that you may overflow with hope by the power of the Holy Spirit" (Romans 15:13).

Find your purpose and destiny

Take the time to carefully consider the course of your life. What are your gifts, talents, and interests? Where are you heading? What will it look like when you get there? Let your imagination take over. Spend time daydreaming about where you want to be in life. Read about it. Study it. Write about it in your journal. Draw it. Paint it. Let your mind run free with the possibilities of what you can attain, what you can be, and what you can accomplish. Transform your imagination into intentions. Act intentionally rather than reacting unconsciously.

"The LORD will vindicate me; your love, LORD, endures forever—do not abandon the works of your hands" (Psalms 138:8).

"'For I know the **plans** I have for you,' declares the Lord, 'plans to **prosper** you and **not to harm** you, plans to **give you hope** and a future'" (Jeremiah 29:11).

PART 2

DESIGN STEP 5

Have you called the right designer for your Home Consultation?
Have you called the Great Designer for your Life Consultation?
Describe the new vision for your overall Home Design.
Describe the new vision for your Life's Design.
What steps do you need to take to complete your Home Design?
What steps do you need to take now to walk into your Life's Design (DESTINY)?
BEAUTIFUL THINGS AWAIT YOU. THE BEST IS YET TO COME!

Remember, you are a beautiful masterpiece created by the greatest Designer ever. I love helping others to learn about their great design. Taking my Free *Inner Beauty Quiz* is a great place to start. Head to the sites below to take the free assessment and to gain access to all my free resources:

Inner Design (Faith-Based Life Coaching):
https://www.restorationroyals.com/free-resources

Interior Design (Online Interior Design Consultations):
https://www.restorationdetails.com/

PART 3

Blazing into the Future

CHAPTER TWELVE
CALLED

IN THE HERE AND NOW

I'd like us to start this part of the book with a powerful reminder of how short our time on earth is, of God's great gift of life from Jesus, and of our freedom to tap into the Holy Spirit—in the here and now.

"But we do see Jesus, who was made lower than the angels for a little while, now crowned with glory and honor because he suffered death, so that by the grace of God he might taste death for everyone" (Hebrews 2:9).

God sent Jesus here for us, and one of the many blessings we received from this was learning how to have an intimate relationship with God, which I know is pivotal in living fully into God's call.

Jesus living as man gave us the opportunity to see how He was in the flesh and **yet also one with God.**

Jesus is our saving grace for more reasons than sacrificing Himself for us. He showed us how to live into God and to

PART 3

live out the call of our Father. Another blessing we received from the time Jesus spent here, in the flesh, was that He knew how hard this would be for us after He left. So, He sent us the Holy Spirit.

- **We can live into God** by getting into the Word and spending time with Him (an intimate connection through His word).
- **We can live with Christ** as we accept Him into our life, and by this we are made new, redeemed (free from footholds).
- **We can live with the Spirit** all day and night, but this too is a matter of free will. I wonder how many of us choose to ACTIVELY do this (tap into this guiding force).

It's all a matter of free will. How many of us live by the Spirit but don't tap into God or live with Christ? How many of us are "saved" but then never walk with the Spirit? And how many of us simply struggle to build an intimate relationship with God?

I want this book to challenge us to do our part and to *Tap into the Trinity*© while we are in the here and now. YOU are called for His purpose, but it's up to you to activate it fully.

"He has saved us and called us to a holy life—not because of **anything we have done** but because of his own purpose and grace. This grace was given us in Christ Jesus before the beginning of time" (2 Timothy 1:9).

I have strategically placed this scripture front and center because years of coaching "everyday people" has made me very aware of the limits by which we allow ourselves to be bound.

Let's challenge some of our limiting thoughts before moving forward.

If your life rests on YOUR works alone then, yes, remain in YOUR greatness alone. Plenty of people do. However, you will also then need to live within YOUR limits. You'll need to love, forgive, move, and absorb as much as YOU can, alone.

But you are a called and saved child of God and you are not alone and never will be, so live into them by *Tapping into the Trinity*©.[2]

Too often I see folks put "called people" into a box of "good people" or "special individuals"—people who are meant for more than everyday living like pastors, missionaries, or those destined to be on stage speaking and moving others in great ways.

Living out your call based on how you and others see yourself, or on how well you've lived your life up until now means you are simply not realizing that anything is possible when connected to God's great plan for you.

God knows our future and is very capable of getting each and every one of us exactly where He wants us. If it were up to us alone, I'm quite convinced Jesus would have been the only one to get it right.

God uses very unlikely individuals in big ways all the time. The folks listed below were not on stage with a huge social media following. They were often seen as nobodies, despicable, or even crazy. However, at some point they focused on their call rather than the world, and that is when amazing things happened in their lives. Let's look at some of the folks God hand-picked.

JACOB WAS A CHEATER (Genesis 27)

The predominant interpretation of Jacob's story is that he was an unconverted cheater who stole his brother Esau's birthright and blessing. Even so, God appeared to him in a dream and converted him. God had big plans for Jacob and He does for you too. We are all sinners and it is never too late for us to be completely changed. I've seen my coaching clients freed of Satan's strongholds in their lives, along with addictions and generational curses that have plagued them for years.

---

[2] © by Niccie Kliegl, 2018

PART 3

No matter what you have done up until now . . .
YOU ARE CALLED AND YOU ARE ENOUGH.

PETER HAD A TEMPER (John 21:15–17)

Throughout the Bible we see how God, Jesus, and many key Christian leaders got angry. What we also know is that anger isn't the problem . . . sin is.

"Be angry and do not sin; do not let the sun go down on your anger" (Ephesians 4:26 ESV).

Sinning in our anger is where **we fall short** and it is the work of the Spirit to help us regain self-control.

"But the fruit of the Spirit is love, joy, peace, forbearance, kindness, goodness, faithfulness, gentleness and self-control. Against such things there is no law" (Galatians 5:22–23).

I love watching individuals learn how to tap into the Holy Spirit. By doing the **30-Day Calling Activation Plan,** you will get into the habit of tapping into the Spirit. We have free will to either live within and under the authority of the world, or of the Spirit. As we learn to live into the Spirit, our whole life transforms for the good. Even our surroundings change for the better.

No matter where you are in your faith journey . . .
YOU ARE CALLED AND YOU ARE ENOUGH.

DAVID HAD AN AFFAIR (2 Samuel 11)

I have coached couples with failed marriages time and time again. These marriages often ended with infidelity yet with God, their lives were repaired and their marriages reunited with a greatness the couple never knew existed. These couples often go on to change the lives of other couples. God is not surprised by our falling prey to the flesh, and He is waiting to restore us and use us for the good of our sisters and brothers . . . for the Kingdom.

We can repent of infidelity, as we can of all sin. As of today, regardless of your past . . .

YOU ARE CALLED AND YOU ARE ENOUGH.

NOAH GOT DRUNK (Genesis 9:21)

There is so much to learn from this story—a story of a man many would hold as great. He was a man as close to perfection as could be found, yet he fell too. We all do. Noah teaches us another lesson about sin. Sin can come from something good when it is not used wisely. God will bless you with great gifts as you learn to step into your calling. However, you need to be prepared; success and plenty are often met with other challenges.

Even the greatest individuals slip up. Sometimes fear of stepping out boldly, knowing that we might fall, holds us back from stepping out at all. My advice here is to have wise counsel (as with two of Noah's three sons) close and ready to support you at all times. It's so much better going out boldly when you have a wise person you can trust to support you rather than shame you.

It's true; with great blessings comes opportunity for a greater fall. So, get wise counsel and GO DO GREAT THINGS.

YOU ARE CALLED AND HE WILL SUPPORT YOU.

JONAH RAN FROM GOD (Jonah 1)

How many of us do this, whether knowingly or not? God is whispering, opening doors, pruning, and preparing you. First of all, are you listening and looking for His guidance and teaching? Next, take a minute and truly ask yourself if you might be running from Him and His call on your life?

I did this. I didn't even know I was doing it. The Holy Spirit spoke to me all the time, even as a child. But I didn't know what it was.

PART 3

Once I figured it out, I didn't know how to step in; I didn't know anyone who had, or even that you could . . . or should. I was doing what everyone around me did. We went to church on Sunday and we prayed, mostly at supper. (Weird, I know. Did we somehow feel supper was more valuable to us or all God cared about?)

Throughout my youthful years and into adulthood I would talk to God, but I didn't know He was talking back; I suppose I never really listened. The Holy Spirit and I talked a lot but I wrote His voice off as intuitiveness and spirituality.

This saddens me, to think of all the people missing out on the Trinity, content to settle on a "higher power," and some even on self alone. Being content with spirituality versus Christianity is a growing and self-limiting danger.

The coaching clients I have worked with who once understood faith in the "higher power" or "spirituality" way were not full of self or even rebuking the one true God. I believe Jesus' last words, "They know not . . ." say it all.

God has huge plans for **you and Him.**

Once I began to step into the Trinity, I was able to see the doors He had been opening for me for years. I learned to hear His voice, which then led me to a whole new lesson on FEAR. Because when you hear God tell you to do something . . . YOU DO IT!

Running from God doesn't stop your call or His desire for you to carry it out.

YOU ARE CALLED AND YOU ARE ENOUGH.

PAUL WAS A MURDERER (1 Corinthians 15:9)

Now you might think, "Good grief, Niccie, this surely doesn't apply to me." Yes, I realize the majority of us have not murdered another human, but I want to challenge us to consider if we have actually *killed* God's plans for our future, *buried* our hope, gifts, and talents.

"And we know that in all things God works for the good **of those who love him,** who have been **called according to his purpose**" (Romans 8:28).

If you feel you have buried great plans that God Himself already breathed life into, do not fear; they are still there waiting for you. Once you dare to step in, HE will work it all out, bringing the plans and you back to life. The God who brought Lazarus back to life can also reignite your call.

Whatever you've buried, fear not, just step in . . . God brings things back to life!

YOU ARE CALLED AND GOD CAN HANDLE IT.

GIDEON WAS INSECURE (Judges 6:33–40) AND THOMAS DOUBTED (John 20:24–29)

Do you feel insecure? Some of us are not only insecure with ourselves, we are also insecure in God. That sounds harsh to say but think about it. If we say we are leaning on God to help us do the impossible and yet we hold back, then we are either doubting God and His ability to work in us (eek!) or we are actually, once again, holding our success captive to our own devices.

Thomas doubted God's love and acceptance for himself, which often results in a flawed view of self, and interferes with one's confidence. Gideon, the Israelite leader, felt insecure about moving forward in his call, so he asked God for two miraculous signs aimed at strengthening his faith. Have you ever tried this? Would you feel weird, like you were doubting God if you asked Him for a sign? To me, Gideon's request was him asking God to increase his faith. If we find ourselves losing confidence in ourselves or God, we need to pray to God to restore that confidence.

Doubting holds you back. As of today, regardless of the level of your confidence, know that YOU ARE CALLED AND GOD IS ALWAYS ENOUGH.

PART 3

MIRIAM WAS A GOSSIP (Numbers 12:1–10)

I include this one because so often our call is clearly connected to sharing our faith. Whether this is within our home, our community, or even in a very public way, it's a lot of pressure and we might let our imperfections hold us back. We might fear others' gossip about us, and being judged as hypocrites. If we judge others, we are more inclined to feel they may judge us.

Although we are not proud of it, gossiping is one of the most common human behaviors. But, like most sin, we often do it without even being aware. The remedy for unintentional sins is to ask God to shed light on them. This can be scary. Honestly, who wants to know how miserable they can be at times? But this is pivotal in wiping out the costly sin of hypocrisy, which can absolutely prevent someone from stepping out boldly and into the public eye.

Ask God to give you eyes to see and a heart of repentance, so hypocrisy dies and humility lives.

YOU ARE CALLED AND YOU ARE ENOUGH.

I covered the most common obstacles experienced by my coaching clients above, but the following also represent common stumbling blocks:

> Sara was impatient . . .
> Elijah moody . . .
> Moses stuttered . . .
> Zaccheus was short . . .
> Abraham was old . . .
> And Lazarus was dead . . .
> Yet God used all of these folks in big ways.
> YOU ARE CALLED.

Now we've put to rest the idea of you not being called or of self-limiting thoughts getting in the way of your call, let's get busy stepping in by learning the key principles of my ***30-Day Calling Activation Plan***.

There are five chapters in the *Blazing into Your Future* part of this book. I will be teaching you how to step into your future boldly, lovingly, and within the call God has on your life. This chapter was meant to open your heart, mind, and soul to the possibilities, and to instill belief in the fact you have been called and you are more than enough when you *Tap into the Trinity*© to do GREAT things.

The next three chapters will teach you a 3-part process for *Tapping into the Trinity*© and for activating great power in your life and the call God has on you. The last chapter will be a 7-day challenge for you to begin the activation. I cannot wait to see how God moves in you and those around you.

I want to leave you with one last biblical truth: **you are predestined.** Let's consider the fact you were actually predestined to do great things for God and the kingdom.

YOU ARE PREDESTINED AND YOU ARE ENOUGH!

"For you created my inmost being; you knit me together **in my mother's womb.** I praise you because I am fearfully and **wonderfully made; your works** are wonderful, **I know that full well**. My frame was not hidden from you when I was made in the secret place, when I was woven together in the depths of the earth. Your eyes saw my unformed body; **all the days ordained for me were written in your book before one of them came to be**" (Psalm 139:13–16).

How has God made you? Do you know it *full well?*

The first time I put the actions of the ***30-Day Calling Activation Plan*** into place was when I was 46 years old. I was a Director of Nursing at the time; God was nudging me to leave this work and start something new. I had no idea what that was so I turned to God, which in itself was new to me. Up until that time, I had only called on God when there was a crisis or if I was immensely grateful.

When we are new at calling out to God, we often miss His guidance and leading. Now that I have an intimate relationship with Him, I hear His voice without even trying. I miss Him and notice when I have distanced myself from Him.

God loves you and loving Him back deeply helps you to hear Him and learn from Him. (No worries, the ***30-Day Calling Activation Plan*** that I will be highlighting will help you to do this.)

"And we know that in all things **God works for the good of those who love him,** who have been called according to his purpose. For those God foreknew **he also predestined** to be conformed to the image of his Son, that he might be the firstborn among many brothers and sisters. **And those he predestined, he also called;** those he called, **he also justified;** those he justified, **he also glorified**" (Romans 8:28–30).

Do you see the pattern in the verses above?

1. Predestined.
2. Called.
3. Justified.
4. Glorified.

God has done His part. He has **predestined** us . . . **and called** us. It is our time to live into the **justification** we've received through our Christ-filled life, and then we need to lean into the Trinity for great works, which will **glorify** God and His kingdom.

YOU AND THE TRINITY ARE MORE THAN ENOUGH!

CHAPTER THIRTEEN
ASK

ASK, SEEK, KNOCK

Ask and it will be given to you; seek and you will find; knock and the door will be opened to you. For everyone who asks receives; the one who seeks finds; and to the one who knocks, the door will be opened.

—Matthew 7:7–8

Ask. Is it really that simple? Yes, it truly is. And, it will be helpful for you to use this chapter to increase your belief in yourself **with the power of the Trinity at work in you**.

Without faith, stepping into the call God has on your life is nearly impossible.

PART 3

Faith in Action

"Now faith is confidence in what we hope for and assurance about what we do not see. This is what the ancients were commended for. **By faith we understand that the universe was formed at God's command, so that what is seen was not made out of what was visible**. By faith Abel brought God a better offering than Cain did. By faith he was commended as righteous, when God spoke well of his offerings. And by faith Abel still speaks, even though he is dead. By faith Enoch was taken from this life, so that he did not experience death: 'He could not be found, because God had taken him away.' For before he was taken, he was commended as one who pleased God. And without faith it is impossible to please God, because anyone who comes to him must believe that he exists and that he rewards those who earnestly seek him" (Hebrews 11:1–6).

Look at these words, the bolded part of the bible verse above: "By faith we understand that the universe was formed at God's command, so that what is seen was not made out of what was visible." It's a very deep thought and speaks so much to the understanding of speaking things into existence. GOD ALREADY SPOKE YOU INTO EXISTENCE. He already predestined you, breathed life into you, and now you, by faith, need to take action and step in.

Stop to think about that. Are you stepping in?

Do you know how?

The 30-Day Calling Activation Plan will help you do that. It's rooted in a 3-Step Process of ASK, SEEK, and KNOCK, based on Matthew 7:7–8.

Ask, Seek, Knock

"Ask and it will be given to you; seek and you will find; knock and the door will be opened to you. For everyone who asks receives; the one who seeks finds; and to the one who knocks, the door will be opened" (Matthew 7:7–8).

So, by faith, let's get busy asking. We have eight clear objectives for asking powerfully:

1. In the name of Jesus Christ.

"And I will do whatever you ask in my name, so that the Father may be glorified in the Son. You may ask me for anything in my name, and I will do it" (John 14:13–14).

Do you pray saying, "In the name of Jesus . . ."?
If not, why?
How often do you ask but leave the doing to yourself?
If so, then are you really asking God?
Why are we told to ask in the name of Jesus?

We are told to ask in the name of Jesus because by doing so, we are stating our belief in God's power to raise Jesus from the dead. The God who did this can do anything. It is our assurance in God and His power to help us.

PART 3

2. According to His will (gifts & talents).

"This is the confidence we have in approaching God: that if we ask anything according to his will, he hears us. And if we know that he hears us—whatever we ask—we know that we have what we asked of him" (1 John 5:14–15).

This can stump us because we don't always know His will. But we can take a few cues from how He has uniquely made us and also how He has been preparing us.

He made you with unique gifts and talents. What are your talents? Don't be shy; you would be surprised at how God has been pruning and refining you. He has plans for you. Others can see your talents. Ask yourself, why do people seek your help for certain things? Don't be caught off guard if it doesn't seem like a calling. Your talents may be used every day and you give them no thought, but once you partner that talent with His divine purpose . . . POW!

Is what you ask for according to His will?
What are some things that come naturally to you?
What comes easy to you?
What gives you energy?

ASK

3. Speak it.

"Hear my prayer, O God; listen to the words of my mouth" (Psalm 54:2).

Have you asked God to hear you? It's a rather humbling feeling; I find it puts me in a seat of honor toward Him. This is very good because as we see God in this place, we are freed to lean into Him with this same awe.

Also, hearing yourself ask God for something takes things to a new level in terms of how serious you are. He hears our voice and listens.

The whole idea of inviting God, the Trinity, into our lives is to become more like them. Think of the power, love, grace, and energy we get from them, the Trinity. God has and does speak things into existence, so call on Him and speak.

Do you know the childhood word for speaking something into existence?

(Throughout the generations we allowed this word—abracadabra—to be misguidedly used. The word is of Hebrew or Aramaic origin, being derived either from the Hebrew words 'ab' (father), 'ben' (son), and 'ruach hakodesh' (holy spirit), or from the Aramaic 'avra kadavra', meaning 'it will be created in my words,' from https://www.phrases.org.uk/meanings/abracadabra.html)

Do you speak life into yourself, your purpose, your capabilities?

(Here is an affirmation video on YOU being chosen, worthy, and called. https://youtu.be/-JeSMnqgd0g)

PART 3

4. Pray for wisdom.

"I keep asking that the God of our Lord Jesus Christ, the glorious Father, may give you the Spirit of wisdom and revelation, so that you may know him better. I pray that the eyes of your heart may be enlightened in order that you may know the hope to which he has called you, the riches of his glorious inheritance in his holy people, and his incomparably great power for us who believe. That power is the same as the mighty strength he exerted when he raised Christ from the dead" (Ephesians 1:17–20).

When we don't know what to do next, we often start trying different things before seeking God and His wisdom or revelation. We look to the person next to us, the person who has "made it" or who has their act together. But calls are unique to the people for whom they are intended. One call doesn't fit all. During these confusing times—and honestly, every day—we need to ask HIM for insight and direction. I so often failed here, slowing myself and my call down by days, weeks, months, and likely years. I missed doors and opened the wrong ones by heading out on my own before asking God what to do next. Now, each morning I ask God what He wants me to do that day.

I ask Him to make my path known, and I tell Him I will follow. I thank Him ahead of time for responding to my request and joyfully look for His answers and clarity.

Are you familiar with the Bible verse found in Ephesians 1:17–20?
Rewrite the verses, replacing "you" with "my" and "I."
Try meditating on this daily.

5. Focus on purpose, not passions.

"When you ask, you do not receive, because you ask with wrong motives, that you may spend what you get on your pleasures" (James 4:3).

Purpose check: this is such an easy step that you can apply it right away. Before you ask God for anything, consider if it is for your own gain or for the kingdom, and to help bring your sisters and brothers home (or maybe a child, or friend).

What are you spending your time and energy on?
Is it bringing Glory to the Kingdom? If so, how?
Have you ever asked God if the things you spend your time on are bringing Him glory?

PART 3

6. Belief in self and God is so important.

"Therefore I tell you, whatever you ask for in prayer, believe that you have received it, and it will be yours" (Mark 11:24).

Oh no, you can't just say . . . you need to believe it. That is why it is so important to understand the *purpose* of what you are doing. God IS invested because it is also HIS purpose for you to succeed. We need to ask for things God wants too . . . then it becomes easy to double down.

Are you ever held back from a cool and exciting dream by lack of belief?

Try seeing the dream differently. See it as God's call, not yours, God's dream, not yours. Do you feel differently now about going out blindly alone, or with Him?

If you do struggle to believe, are you doubting God's ability or your own?

7. Faith, more than belief.

"If you believe, you will receive whatever you ask for in prayer" (Matthew 21:22).

Faith is **the precursor to action**. Belief is a thought. "I believe God raised Jesus from the dead," versus "I have faith that God raised Jesus from the dead, so I will . . ."

List the actions you will take, based on the faith of what you believe.
So, I will:
So, I will:
So, I will:

PART 3

8. Believe when you don't believe.

"Immediately the boy's father exclaimed, 'I do believe; help me overcome my unbelief!'" (Mark 9:24).

Isn't this awesome? There will likely be times when you simply can't muster up the courage to go all in. Have you ever been in a situation where you were afraid, but you did it anyway? Maybe the first time you jumped off a diving board? Got married? Had kids? You do it because something in you reasons your way into thinking it will be alright. You can do it.

This is the most obedient, faith-filled ask God could ever hear—to be full of human doubt, yet surrender that doubt to lean into His Omni-call on our life.

> Looking back at times when God was there for us increases our faith. This is why the sabbath is so important. It's a time to look back on God's work in our lives and for us to acknowledge, "It is good." This builds trust for the next time.
>
> List a few things God has done for you. Think hard; many of us overlook all the help He has provided.

"Ask and it will be given to you; seek and you will find; knock and the door will be opened to you. For everyone who asks receives; the one who seeks finds; and to the one who knocks, the door will be opened" (Matthew 7:7–8).

By faith, ASK.

CHAPTER FOURTEEN
SEEK

ASK, **SEEK**, KNOCK

Ask and it will be given to you; **seek and you will find;** *knock and the door will be opened to you. For everyone who asks receives; the one who seeks finds; and to the one who knocks, the door will be opened.*

—*Matthew 7:7–8*

Seek what? Well, much to our dismay we shouldn't seek **the call** alone. Check out this verse:

"Look to the Lord and his strength; seek his face always" (1 Chronicles 16:11).

Seek **His strength and His face, His presence,** is what the verse says. Why would this even be said if all we had to do was ask God and have faith? I see it all the time with my coaching clients. This is what separates the pack. Those who quickly learn to keep their eyes rightly focused on the LORD

PART 3

begin to power through obstacles, leap forward with grace, and blaze into the future with their souls on fire. This is what I want for you.

What do you seek, look for, turn to, or desire, with all your heart?

"You will seek me and find me when you seek me with all your heart" (Jeremiah 29:13).

So let me walk you through the five aspects of seeking God with all your heart, right out of the ***30-Day Calling Activation Plan***, to get you started.

#1 IN PRAYER:

"Let us then approach God's throne of grace with confidence, so that we may receive mercy and find grace to help us in our time of need" (Hebrews 4:16).

How can we approach the throne, the King, and pray confidently? A common tool for praying is to use the acronym P.R.A.Y.: **P**raise, **R**epent, **A**ccess, and **Y**ield.

PRAISE: We're to enter His gates with thanksgiving and His courts with praise (see Psalm 100:4). Sit quietly and thank God for who He is and what He has done.

REPENT: A sober reminder comes from Psalm 66:18: "If I had cherished sin in my heart, the Lord would not have listened." A spiritual cleansing is needed in order to come nearer to the throne of God.

ACCESS: We're not telling God anything new. "All my longings lie open before you, Lord; my sighing is not hidden from you" (Psalm 38:9). Even so, He gives us access to talk to Him about our needs and frustrations. We need to call upon the Holy Spirit to intercede for us as we connect with all our heart.

YIELD: Humbly bringing our prayer list before God indicates our trust that He is able, and He will—in His time and way—show us the direction we should go (see Psalm

143:8). We can be confident when we pray according to His will (1 John 5:14).

Do not worry about your experience in praying because God loves a simple and sincere prayer, telling us to not babble on with many words (Matthew 6:7).

A very powerful way to pray with some direction is to pray His promises from the Word back to Him. Claim your position as His child, His sovereignty over you and the world, His power over darkness, and His love and care for those who love Him. Remember to get to His Word, the Bible, and to call on the Holy Spirit to help it come to life in you and for you, and claim its truth as you pray.

"In the beginning was the Word, and the Word was with God, and the Word was God" (John 1:1).

I'm very passionate about teaching the Bible to people. I had a hard time getting disciplined in reading daily at first, and in understanding what the early books in the Bible were teaching. At first, it seemed too overwhelming.

But I know personally—and have seen with ALL my coaching clients—the power the Word holds, beginning with life transformation and then fully living out our call. So, I invest a lot of my time helping others get into the habit of reading the Word, praying, and praising God. My private community calls this having a "Heart of Habitue," the habit and heart to know and follow God.

I hold weekend retreats called W.O.W. (Will of the Word), during which I teach the Bible to large and small groups of women. In addition, I take the Legacy Leaders (my private online community of growing Christian Leaders) through the Bible each year by reading to them a section each day and then teaching how it applies to our lives.

God will continue to teach us through the written word. It often starts by hearing a great verse, leaning into a few that resonate, then desiring to learn and study, and ultimately to use God (His Word) to do great work for the kingdom. I'll

PART 3

share a story of when this deeper level of Bible reading took root for me.

One night, the written Word and my prayer life combined out of desperation, and it was powerful to say the least. My best advice is to take a problem or worry and look up several Bible verses on that topic. Copy them onto paper and be sure to rephrase them with your name or another's name (if they are part of your request) and make them into statements. In this way, you are repeating back to God a promise that He has made as a statement for a loved one, thus commanding its truth. In this way, you are leaning into the promises of God. This will bring you great peace.

Something else I learned this night while praying with everything I had, was the significance in the posture of prayer. Instinctively, my body began doing the only thing it knew to do, which was going back and forth from my knees to bowing and back again. Finally, exhausted, I surrendered to the great work God promised to do, and went to my Bible and studied up on bowing while praying. It was then I learned that bowing is only one of many positions.

As children, we learn to bow our head or even kneel, but I had no idea of the power in our posture. My body simply did what it had to do: going from a child's pose to bowing, to kneeling, and back. Now I could see how these positions lined up with humility, releasing control, and showing reverence. In this prayer, I had to humble myself and lean into God's power; there wasn't a thing I could do at the moment but pray and I had to release control to God. If I didn't allow myself to trust Him and to revere Him with His power, I'd be wasting my efforts. I prayed with all my heart that night and He showed up big time.

What is happening in your life now that you need big help with?

What have YOU done to call on God thus far?

Did you do it out on your own, or did you invite God along?

PART 3

Different Ways to Pray

Bowing on your knees—Humility to the Almighty
"For this reason I bow my knees before the Father" (Ephesians 3:14 ESV).

Walking–Building momentum
"Elisha turned away and walked back and forth in the room and then got on the bed and stretched out on him once more. The boy sneezed seven times and opened his eyes" (2 Kings 4:35).

Child's pose—Releasing control, safe under the Father
"I praise you because I am fearfully and wonderfully made; your works are wonderful, I know that full well" (Psalm 139:14).

Out loud—Proclaiming truth with need to be heard
"This poor man called, and the Lord heard him; he saved him out of all his troubles" (Psalm 34:6).

Silently—Connected in Spirit
"Hannah was praying in her heart, and her lips were moving but her voice was not heard" (1 Samuel 1:13).

Hands lifted—Surrendering to God's sovereign power
"Therefore I want the men everywhere to pray, lifting up holy hands without anger or disputing" (1 Timothy 2:8).

Head bowed—Showing reverence and respect
"The man bowed his head and worshiped the Lord" (Genesis 24:26 ESV).

Prostrate—Ultimate act of submission and worship
"Going a little farther, he fell with his face to the ground and prayed, "My Father, if it is possible, may this cup be taken from me. Yet not as I will, but as You will" (Matthew 26:39).

Standing—Invited to approach
"And when you stand praying, if you hold anything against anyone, forgive them, so that your Father in heaven may forgive you your sins" (Mark 11:25).

I've been very passionate about growing my prayer life. Two things I weave into the ***30-Day Calling Activation Plan*** are the importance of love and community in our prayer life and in living out our call.

Love is necessary to reach intimacy with God. "Whoever does not love does not know God, because God is love" (1 John 4:8). Try to think of prayer as a way to show your love to God. Think of your own children and how loved you feel when your child talks with you and seeks you for advice.

In Matthew 6:13–14, Jesus impresses upon us the need for a loving, forgiving spirit. Have you given much thought to there being different spirits? There are. We say things like, "She is so mean-spirited," but I think we fail to realize the truth in this. We either walk in the world where we are prey to Satan and those spirits, or with the Holy Spirit where there is protection from those spirits as well as power beyond belief.

With God-partnered living, we are not only able to tap into God's protection but we are also blessed with the Holy Spirit who is loving, patient, kind, good, gentle, faithful, peaceful, joyful, and full of self-control (Galatians 5:22–23). As we tap into the Trinity we pull in closer to God's love, the Holy Spirit's fruit, and Jesus' saving grace, thus finding ourselves in a beautiful, intimate place with God.

With regard to community, we must remember that "where two or three gather in my name, there am I with them" (Matthew 18:20). Prayer is a tool used often by Jesus. He taught the disciples how to pray in a way that would bring them close to God and His insight, power, and strength. I can only imagine how amazing it would have been to pray with Jesus in those days. Think of the unity and power the disciples must have captured as they joined together with Him in prayer. We each carry different spiritual gifts and when we pray together, all our spirits unite to send out prayers of great magnitude.

#2 PRAISE MUSIC

"Yet a time is coming and has now come when the true worshipers will worship the Father in the Spirit and in truth, for they are the kind of worshipers the Father seeks" (John 4:23).

Throughout the Bible, we learn of the instinctive response to sing and shout praises of joy. We are encouraged to lift up our praises with one voice. The angels sang together, the people sang together, and we sing together still today.

Many times, the music ministry component of a worship service is a heartfelt surrender at the beginning allowing us to receive the Word as the service continues. This too is an act of discipline, growth, and power for many.

Find the music that sings to your soul, be it old hymns, piano, bands, or big church anthems. Begin to play them in your car, on your cell phone or in your home so you learn what fills you up, prepares your heart, brings peace, joy, and energy. Allow yourself to feel the music and even break out in dance if it moves you. I'm a dancer. You can find me most every day while my coffee brews, or while I wait on the microwave, dancing in circles to sounds of praise strumming through my home, morning to night. Throughout the Bible, we see the powerful expression of praising God through music and dance.

#3 WISE COUNSEL

"For lack of guidance a nation falls, but victory is won through many advisers" (Proverbs 11:14).

"The way of fools seems right to them, but the wise listen to advice" (Proverbs 12:15).

"Listen to advice and accept discipline, and at the end you will be counted among the wise. Many are the plans in a person's heart, but it is the Lord's purpose that prevails" (Proverbs 19:20–21).

"Plans fail for lack of counsel, but with many advisors they succeed" (Proverbs 15:22).

When stepping out in blind faith, use the Holy Spirit and check the fruit to be sure you are tapped into the Trinity.

"I am the true vine, and my Father is the gardener. He cuts off every branch in me that bears no fruit, while every branch in me that does bear fruit he prunes so that it will be even more fruitful. You are already clean because of the word I have spoken to you. Remain in me, as I also remain in you. No branch can bear fruit by itself; it must remain in the vine. Neither can you bear fruit unless you remain in me. I am the vine; you are the branches. If you remain in me and I in you, you will bear much fruit; apart from me you can do nothing" (John 15:1–27).

Checking the fruit is one of the most powerful ways to see if you are walking with the Spirit or pushing through with the world. Even during hard times, God finds ways to bless us out of hardships.

"You intended to harm me, but God intended it for good to accomplish what is now being done, the saving of many lives" (Genesis 50:20).

I don't think Christians lean on the Holy Spirit as much as we should, or understand the drastic difference of walking in the world or with the Spirit. The thing is, there are all sorts of spirits around. If we are not walking with the HOLY SPIRIT, we are at liberty of joining up with others, even without knowing.

God will use the Holy Spirit through others to help you along the way, but so will Satan, so you need to be careful about who you are partnering with and listening to. We are told to encourage and raise each other up, so SEEK wise counsel. If you want to go deeper on how to live with the Spirit and use that to step into your call, study the book of Romans. Part of the ***30-Day Calling Activation Plan*** came from Romans 9–11. I have a free *24-Day Called Conquerors* mini-course on my https://nicciekliegl.com/free-resources/ page, which you can access to work through privately or in a group.

#4 BRINGS GOD GLORY

Part of seeking God is steering clear of places that are not divine or intended for you and your call. It's appropriate to look at this now, right after discussing how to seek wise counsel. It is sometimes hard to know what is good for you and what exactly God is asking of you.

"So whether you eat or drink or whatever you do, do it all for the glory of God" (1 Corinthians 10:31).

This is honestly the foolproof check: would God do this, eat that, partner with him/her, give to that?

Every day, I hear others say they would follow God, do God's work, and go where He is leading—if they could only hear Him. Not knowing what God is asking us to do can be a horrible feeling. "If God would simply tell me what to do, I'd do it." Right?

Probably the most helpful step in living fully into our call is to simply *step in*, following or being obedient to the nudges you feel. Even if you don't get it right first time, He will redirect and bless your efforts if your heart is right. This is a practice that helps those who feel tentative about how God is calling them be assured they are on the right track. God will bless the work we do as long as that work brings Him glory.

Do a little personal check each morning and night. Each morning, ask yourself if the things on your schedule for the day will bring God glory. Then ask yourself at the end of your day, "Have the things I've done today brought God glory?" This is one easy tip tucked into your journal for Day 10 of the ***30-Day Calling Activation Plan*** that will help you tighten up your day, step into your call, and bless your life greatly.

#5 SABBATH SPACE

"By the seventh day God had finished the work he had been doing; so on the seventh day he rested from all his work. Then God blessed the seventh day and made it holy, because on it he rested from all the work of creating that he had done" (Genesis 2:2–3).

Do you recognize the good and see God's hand, strength, and power in your life? If you are not slowing down enough to look back and see how He has saved you, loved you, and guided you, it will be hard to lean into all the power He offers. We often write off God's great work as coincidence, our own greatness, or that of others helping us along.

It's important to find a rhythm of rigor, rest, reflect, and raising up, which allows us to tap into **Trinity Power**. The ***30-Day Calling Activation Plan*** will teach you a wonderful rhythm to your life of working hard for the Lord, resting well, reflecting on God's presence, and raising Him up—along with yourself and others—all for the Kingdom and His purpose.

RIGOR: Laboring in your sweet spot replaces day-to-day work with a flow that goes from God to you with in-sync passion and purpose. Focus and high performance come easily because you are doing His work with His purpose for your life, and He is directly helping you.

REST: Periods of rest enable needed recovery for your mind, body, and soul before you go back at it with gusto. "Then, because so many people were coming and going that they did not even have a chance to eat, he said to them, 'Come with me by yourselves to a quiet place and get some rest'" (Mark 6:31).

REFLECT: Without looking back, we can miss out on recognizing the work that has been done. This can make us weary in spirit and strip our mind of the help God has provided, which then suppresses the level of faith we will have in God doing great things in us for the future. In Jude 1:5–7, Jude looks back on the powerful things God has done, which gives him courage to act boldly in faith. If you want to increase your faith fast, this is a necessary step.

RAISE: This is where we own our position, praise God for His, and raise up our hands in surrender to His next call, while we thank God for the growth and movement accomplished. God wants us confident in what we hope for and yet do not see (see Hebrews 11:1).

CHAPTER FIFTEEN
KNOCK

ASK, SEEK, **KNOCK**

Ask and it will be given to you; seek and you will find; **knock and the door will be opened to you.** *For everyone who asks receives; the one who seeks finds; and to the one who knocks, the door will be opened.*

—*Matthew 7:7–8*

Knock and the door will be opened to you. To knock is a request for admission when the way is closed. The door blocks our way but God will open it, allowing us and Him to flow in and out (heaven on earth). To knock is us taking imperfect action here on earth as we continue to do our best.

We can force the door open, and we often do; it's our choice and we have free will. When, as God-loving individuals, we do life alone or go out ahead of Him, we miss the divine opportunities to move swiftly and effectively through life and into our call.

PART 3

From the beginning of time, we've moved in a pattern of our independent folly and God's unfailing faithfulness. We have learned hard lessons from going out on our own, and focusing our eyes on the prize over the Presenter.

In the ASK part of activating your calling, we focused our mind, ideas, and intentions on God. In the SEEK part, we mastered the art of Tapping into the Trinity©. Now, as we learn more about the KNOCK part of activating your calling, we learn how to take imperfect action, united with God through a tangible (physical) request—the knock. Here we surrender our independent action and wait for His divine invitation.

Until "that day," the day when Christ comes and we enter the royal gates, we are not perfect. But we do get to call on the Perfector. We are encouraged to continuously present our sinful, confused, and often misdirected intentions before Him, where God's authority, wisdom, power, righteousness, and glory can do their work here on earth.

There is no time limit on His great gift, but we need to be willing to accept it. It's been here from the beginning of time; it is here today, and will be tomorrow . . .

If we so choose.

"*Kairos* is God's dimension—one not marked by the past, the present, or the future. When Jesus came, it was a fulfillment of promises past, a cosmic collision of the sacred and secular. It was an intersection of the holy will of God and the stubborn ways of man—a perfect moment."[3]

It's a beautiful place—allowing our imperfect self to align with Him in a flow of imperfect action toward our call, being refined, guided, and boosted because we have invited Him into it and He has invited us into His presence.

---

[3] Living a Kairos Life in a Chronos World
Blog / Produced by The High Calling
https://www.theologyofwork.org/the-high-calling/blog/living-kairos-life-chronos-world

So, how do we surrender to this *kairos* gift each and every day? How do we step in and knock? Ephesians 4:22–24 is one of my favorite passages in the Bible and quickly becomes the "go to" message for many of my coaching clients. Learning to surrender is powerful and life-giving.

". . . to put off your old self, which is being corrupted by its deceitful desires; to be made new in the attitude of your minds; and to put on the new self, created to be like God in true righteousness and holiness" (Ephesians 4:22–24).

The battle for us, living out our call here on earth, is that there is sin here. Its goal is to pull us away from God and His call on our lives, which always leads back to us helping the unbeliever find their way back home. Satan knows if we learn to confidently go out with God, he's in trouble and will be defeated.

"He said: "Listen, King Jehoshaphat and all who live in Judah and Jerusalem! This is what the Lord says to you: '**Do not be afraid or discouraged because of this vast army. For the battle is not yours, but God's**. Tomorrow march down against them. They will be climbing up by the Pass of Ziz, and you will find them at the end of the gorge in the Desert of Jeruel. You will not have to fight this battle. **Take up your positions; stand firm and see the deliverance the Lord will give you**, Judah and Jerusalem. **Do not be afraid; do not be discouraged. Go out to face them tomorrow, and the Lord will be with you**" (2 Chronicles 20:15–17).

Satan doesn't want us learning how to surrender our imperfect ways, knowing this allows us to more freely tap into Trinitary power. As we surrender our old self, the door opens to a new self. It must exhaust him horribly as we learn to continuously lay our transgressions down and surrender our sinful manners that hold us back.

I love to see us lean into Christ's gift, to learn to navigate this flow of old self to new self, so we can be renewed and soar like eagles, run and not grow weary, walk and not faint (see Isaiah 40:31).

PART 3

Here is a tool that I use when teaching my clients to live freely, away from the footholds with which Satan tries to bind us. This teaching is deeply rooted in the *knock* portion of the ***30-Day Calling Activation Plan***.

Download and begin using it today: https://nicciekliegl.com/free-resources/

We sometimes give ourselves too much credit, saying that we get in our own way of great success and gain. But I want you to be wise. Satan doesn't want us to succeed in our call; he is in the business of lying, killing, and destroying. Your call will do the opposite; it will bring our sisters and brothers into the light. So, when there is resistance or a setback, be wise and . . .

> **Put On the Armor of God**
>
> —Ephesians 6:10–20:
>
> "Finally, be strong in the Lord and in his mighty power. Put on the full armor of God, so that you can take your stand against the devil's schemes. For our struggle is not against flesh and blood, but against the rulers, against the authorities, against the powers of this dark world and against the spiritual forces of evil in the heavenly realms. Therefore put on the full armor of God, so that when the day of evil comes, you may be able to stand your ground, and after you have done everything, to stand. Stand firm then, with the belt of truth buckled around your waist, with the breastplate of righteousness . . .

To download my image of the Armor of God, head to https://nicciekliegl.com/free-resources/

As we learn the flow of surrender and knock, we begin to live into all Christ has already done for us, into what the Holy Spirit is whispering to us, and into the power that God has invited us to. Pray this prayer daily as you learn to step into His strength.

PART 3

PRAYER FOR SPIRITUAL STRENGTH

"For this reason I kneel before the Father, from whom every family in heaven and on earth derives its name. I pray that out of his glorious riches he may strengthen you with power through his Spirit in your inner being, so that Christ may dwell in your hearts through faith. And I pray that you, being rooted and established in love, may have power, together with all the Lord's holy people, to grasp how wide and long and high and deep is the love of Christ, and to know this love that surpasses knowledge—that you may be filled to the measure of all the fullness of God. Now to him who is able to do immeasurably more than all we ask or imagine, according to his power that is at work within us, to him be glory in the church and in Christ Jesus throughout all generations, for ever and ever! Amen" (Ephesians 3:14–21).

YOU CAN KNOCK NOW, EVERY DAY, EVERY HOUR, AND EVERY MINUTE.

How can you start to step into His presence (through your prayer life, praise, wise counsel, work, sabbath)?

How can you start to step into His presence (through praising God)?

How can you start to step into His presence (through wise counsel)?

How can you start to step into His presence (through your work)?

How can you start to step into His presence (through practicing the sabbath)?

CHAPTER SIXTEEN
ACTIVATED

IN THE HERE AND NOW

I am so excited to use this last chapter to actually start you on your 30-day journey to activating the call God has on your life. The *30-Day Calling Activation Plan* is designed to give you manageable, incremental action steps toward activating your call.

The plan is chronological, first addressing Angela's restorative teaching from *Burning off the Past*, then Barb's creative wisdom from *Lighting up the Present*, and finally, my leading from *Blazing into the Future*. No matter where you are in your faith journey, know that . . .

The God of *kairos* is not bound by space or time. **He has appointed us, for the here and now**, in preparation for the fulfillment of scripture. You are called and the 30-day journey helps you step in fully. See the following pages for the first five days, which will open the eyes of your heart to His glorious inheritance and to the immeasurable power at work in you (us), and to all those who believe.

". . . that the God of our Lord Jesus Christ, the glorious Father, may give you the Spirit of wisdom and revelation, so that you may know him better. I pray that the eyes of your heart may be enlightened in order that you may know the hope to which he has called you, the riches of his glorious inheritance in his holy people, and his incomparably great power for us who believe. That power is the same as the mighty strength he exerted when he raised Christ from the dead and seated him at his right hand in the heavenly realms" (Ephesians 1:17–20).

My advice is to start today with day one, and to do one day at a time. The steps seem simple and fast-moving but they are powerful.

We want you to be committed and engaged with your heart as you think about the day's action item, building on each day.

Blessings friends,

YOU ARE CALLED.

01 TRUTH
THE TRUTH WILL SET YOU FREE

SO JESUS SAID TO THE JEWS WHO HAD BELIEVED HIM, "IF YOU ABIDE IN MY WORD YOU ARE TRULY MY DISCIPLES, AND YOU WILL KNOW THE TRUTH, AND THE TRUTH WILL SET YOU FREE."

John 8:31-32

1. HOW SATISFIED ARE YOU IN YOUR CURRENT JOB/CAREER?

2. HOW CONTENT ARE YOU WITH YOUR LIFE?

3. DO YOU FEEL YOU ARE MAKING A DIFFERENCE IN YOUR SURROUNDINGS?

4. HOW DO YOU FEEL ABOUT YOURSELF?

5. HOW DO YOU FEEL ABOUT YOUR CURRENT HEALTH?

6. HOW AWARE OF YOUR SPIRITUAL GIFTS ARE YOU?

7. HOW EASY IS IT FOR YOU TO MAKE DECISIONS?

8. HOW OFTEN DO YOU FEEL YOU KNOW WHAT GOD IS ASKING OF YOU, OR YOU FEEL THE HOLY SPIRIT NUDGING YOU?

9. HOW WELL DO YOU SLEEP AT NIGHT?

10. DO YOU FIND PAST MISTAKES HOLD YOU BACK FROM PROGRESSING IN LIFE?

11. DO YOU STRUGGLE TO FORGIVE ANYONE IN YOUR LIFE?

12. HOW OFTEN DO YOU FIND YOURSELF PRAYING?

13. HOW COMPELLED ARE YOU TO HELP OTHERS?

Take the Spiritual Gifts Test https://giftstest.com/ to see some natural gifts today. We'll do it again at the end of the 40-days. You'll be shocked at your growth!

02 POSSIBILITY
THE POSSIBILITY LIES IN OUR WILL

WHO SAVED US AND CALLED US TO A HOLY CALLING, NOT BECAUSE OF OUR WORKS BUT BECAUSE OF HIS OWN PURPOSE AND GRACE, WHICH HE GAVE US IN CHRIST JESUS BEFORE THE AGES BEGAN.

2 Timothy 1:9

1. DO YOU BELIEVE GOD SAVED YOU SPECIFICALLY?
   _____
   _____

2. DO YOU BELIEVE HE HAS CALLED YOU TO A HOLY CALLING? IF SO WHAT IS IT?
   _____
   _____
   _____
   _____

3. IF HE CALLS US FOR HIS PURPOSE, WHAT IS HIS ULTIMATE PURPOSE?
   _____
   _____
   _____

4. WHY DO YOU THINK THIS VERSE ALSO SAYS, "AND GRACE"?
   _____
   _____

JOURNAL HERE ANY AREAS YOU FEEL NEED GOD'S GRACE, OR YOUR GRACE, IN ORDER TO MOVE FORWARD INTO YOUR CALL FULLY.
   _____
   _____
   _____
   _____

5. WHY IS IT IMPORTANT TO REMEMBER IT IS THE SAME POWER THAT RAISED JESUS THAT IS CALLING US?
   _____
   _____

6. IN WHAT WAYS DO YOU FEEL INADEQUATE FOR GOD TO USE?
   _____
   _____

7. DO YOU ASK GOD REGULARLY TO EQUIP YOU? _____
WHAT ACTIONS ARE YOU TAKING TO LEARN FROM GOD, JESUS, AND THE HOLY SPIRIT?
   _____
   _____

6. IF YOU LIVE INTO TRINITARIAN POWER, WHAT CAN STAND IN YOUR WAY?
   _____
   _____

7. UP UNTIL NOW, HOW HAVE YOU BEEN LIVING INTO THE POWER OF JESUS?
   _____
   _____

Watch this video I made to inspire you to step into your call at
https://youtu.be/-JeSMnqgd0g

03 HOPE
THE CHOICE OF HOPE IS ALWAYS THERE

JESUS IS OUR SAVING GRACE FOR MORE REASON THAN SACRIFICING HIMSELF FOR US. HE SHOWED US HOW TO LIVE INTO GOD AND TO LIVE OUT THE CALL OF OUR FATHER. ANOTHER BLESSING WE RECEIVED FROM THE TIME JESUS SPENT HERE IN THE FLESH, WAS THAT HE KNEW HOW HARD THIS WOULD BE FOR US AFTER HE LEFT. SO HE LEFT US THE HOLY SPIRIT.

WE CAN LIVE INTO GOD BY GETTING TO THE WORD AND SPENDING TIME WITH HIM (AN INTIMATE CONNECTION THROUGH HIS WORD).

WE CAN LIVE WITH CHRIST AS WE ACCEPT HIM INTO OUR LIFE, AND BY THIS WE ARE MADE NEW, REDEEMED (FREE FROM FOOTHOLDS).

AND WE CAN LIVE WITH THE SPIRIT ALL DAY AND NIGHT, BUT THIS TOO IS A MATTER OF FREE WILL AND I WONDER HOW MANY OF US CHOSE TO ACTIVELY DO THIS (TAP INTO HIS GUIDING FORCE).

It's all a matter of free will.

HAVE YOU GIVEN MUCH THOUGHT TO THERE BEING TWO PLACES WHICH WE WALK IN, LIVE IN?

_____
_____
_____
_____

RECOGNIZE

IF SO WHERE HAVE YOU BEEN WALKING? AND DESCRIBE HOW.

_____
_____
_____
_____

REMOVE

TODAY, I WANT YOU TO REMOVE SOMETHING YOU HAVE BEEN DOING THAT PULLS YOU AWAY FROM THE SPIRIT. REMEMBER, ANYTHING THAT ISN'T NOBLE, EXCELLENT, PRAISEWORTHY, OR ADMIRABLE TO GOD IS A GOOD PLACE TO START. WRITE IT DOWN HERE. (PHIL 4:8)

_____
_____
_____

REPLACE

I WOULD ALSO LIKE FOR YOU TO REPLACE THAT BRAIN SPACE WITH SOMETHING THAT IS IN ALIGNMENT WITH THE SPIRIT. THIS ONE CYCLE OF "RECOGNIZE AND REPLACE" WILL BE LIFE-GIVING. BY REMOVING AND REPLACING TOGETHER, YOU TWO-FOLD ITS EFFECT ON YOUR LIFE. WRITE DOWN THE NEW ACTION YOU WILL BE TAKING.

_____
_____
_____
_____
_____
_____
_____

04 KILLER
THE ENEMY KILLS YOUR DREAM, NOT YOU

GOD USES VERY UNLIKELY INDIVIDUALS IN BIG WAYS ALL THE TIME. THESE PEOPLE WERE NOT ON STAGE WITH A HUGE SOCIAL MEDIA FOLLOWING. THE FOLKS LISTED BELOW WERE OFTEN SEEN AS NOBODIES, DESPICABLE, OR EVEN CRAZY. HOWEVER, AT SOME POINT, THEIR FOCUS WAS ON THE CALL, NOT THE WORLD, AND THAT IS WHEN AMAZING THINGS HAPPENED IN THEIR LIVES.

Let's name them one by one.

THE ENEMY TEMPTS US WITH THE FLESH AND TRICKS US WITH THE "EASY WAY OUT" ONLY TO LATER LABEL US WHEN WE FALL PREY.

IF WE ARE NOT CAREFUL, WE CAN LET HIS LIES KILL OUR DREAMS, HOPES, AND THE FUTURE GOD HAS INTENDED FOR US AND HIS PEOPLE. (JEREMIAH 29:11)

JOURNAL HERE YOUR PAST SINS. AND DON'T BE SHY TO RECALL THEM. NAME THEM AND WRITE THEM DOWN. THIS ONLY BRINGS THEM INTO THE LIGHT, REMOVING SATAN'S POWER OVER YOU BECAUSE OF THEM AS WE LAY THEM AT THE CROSS.

NAME THEM HERE, ONE BY ONE, AND REMOVE THE ENEMY'S FOOTHOLD.

_____
_____
_____
_____
_____
_____
_____
_____
_____
_____
_____
_____

ONE OF THE MOST POWERFUL THINGS WE CAN DO AS WE LAY OUR SINS AT THE FOOT OF THE CROSS IS TO THANK JESUS. (THIS ACT NAMES HIM AS YOUR SAVIOR WHERE TRUE TRANSFORMATION BEGINS.) **I WANT YOU TO STEP INTO YOUR CALL FULLY AND THIS WILL STRENGTHEN AND FREE YOU BEFORE YOU GO ALL IN.**

WRITE OUT A SIMPLE PRAYER OF GRATITUDE HERE. DO NOT GET HUNG UP ON STRUCTURE OR ACCURACY. ANY HEARTFELT PRAYER IS HEARD.

...IN EVERYTHING BY PRAYER AND SUPPLICATION WITH THANKSGIVING LET YOUR REQUESTS BE MADE KNOWN TO GOD (PHILIPPIANS 4:6).

_____
_____
_____
_____

NOW WHAT IS THE DREAM THAT GOD SET IN YOU, MAYBE AS A CHILD, LAST MONTH, OR MAYBE IT IS STILL BREWING?

_____
_____
_____

Watch this brief inspirational video on forgiveness youtube link

05 STAND FIRM
THE NAME OF JESUS IS OUR STRONG TOWER

THERE ARE 8 CLEAR OBJECTIVES FOR STANDING POWERFULLY AGAINST ANYTHING. THE FIRST BEING TO STAND FIRM IN THE NAME OF JESUS CHRIST.

> *Whatever you ask in my name, this I will do, that the Father may be glorified in the Son. If you ask me anything in my name, I will do it.* John 14:13-14 (ESV)

HOW OFTEN DO YOU ASK OR PRAY FOR HELP BUT THEN LEAVE THE DOING TO YOURSELF?
_____

DO YOU KNOW HOW TO ENGAGE GOD INTO YOUR PLANS?
_____

ONE POWERFUL WAY IS THROUGH MEDITATING ON BIBLE VERSES AND THROUGH POSITIVE AFFIRMATIONS MADE FROM SCRIPTURE:

TO SPEAK IT.

I WOULD HAVE ONLY CONSIDERED THE TERM ABRACADABRA AS AN IGNORANT HOCUS POCUS OF OUR YOUTH. THEN AS I PREPARED A BIBLE STUDY ON 'WORDS OF AFFIRMATION' AND GOD SPEAKING THINGS INTO EXISTENCE I FOUND THIS...

NO ONE IS SURE AS TO THE ORIGIN OF THE STRANGE WORD 'ABRACADABRA' NEVERTHELESS, THERE ARE SEVERAL THEORIES NOTING THE WORD IS OF HEBREW OR ARAMAIC ORIGIN, BEING DERIVED EITHER FROM THE HEBREW WORDS 'AB' (FATHER), 'BEN' (SON), AND 'RUACH HAKODESH' (HOLY SPIRIT), OR FROM THE ARAMAIC 'AVRA KADAVRA', MEANING 'IT WILL BE CREATED IN MY WORDS'
HTTPS://WWW.PHRASES.ORG.UK/MEANINGS/ABRACADABRA.HTML

SO WHILE MANY PRACTICE POSITIVE SELF-TALK, AND OTHERS MEDITATE ON THINGS OF THE WORLD, I HAVE SEEN THE AMAZING POWER OF SPEAKING GOD'S WORD OVER OUR LIFE. THE HOLY SPIRIT ACTIVATES WITHIN THE WORD MAKING IT A LIVING WORD... GOD'S WORD LIVING IN YOU - SO SPEAK TRUTH.

TAKE THREE AREAS YOU STRUGGLE WITH. GO FIND SCRIPTURE THAT SPEAKS GOD'S POWER OVER YOUR LIFE IN THAT AREA. (YOU CAN DO THIS BY A SIMPLE GOOGLE SEARCH OF 'BIBLE VERSES ON...'). THEN WRITE THEM BELOW AND BEGIN SPEAKING THEM OVER YOURSELF DAILY. PUT YOUR NAME INTO THE VERSES TOO.

_____
_____
_____
_____

_____
_____
_____
_____

_____
_____
_____
_____

Meet the authors

Angela Crist, author of *Kairos Time*, inner healing minister, coach, ordained apostle/pastor, entrepreneur, and speaker who helps women burn off their past in order to climb higher in the Lord.

Angela has a burning passion to see the body of Christ walk in wholeness and to make *JESUS* famous as people step out of the chains that bind them and step into their full purpose, calling, and destiny. She teaches what it looks like to be a martyr for the Lord by dying to self every day, and laying down your life for the One who paid it all on Calvary.

Many appreciate her for her humor, infectious deep laugh, and ability to keep it real by discussing topics that often aren't discussed within the four walls of a church—real-life issues.

Angela is married to her best friend, Pastor David Crist, and lives in beautiful central Ohio. Together they have 6 grown children—3 boys and 3 girls—2 adorable grandsons, and future littles on the way.

You can learn more about Angela by visiting her website at angelacrist.me or finding her ministry group on Facebook, *The Destiny Seekers*.

DESTINY SEEKERS COACHING
WITH ANGELA CRIST

LIFE ADVANCEMENT

INNER HEALING

SPEAKER   **COACH**    **SUBSCRIPTION COMMUNITY**

STEP INTO YOUR FULL POTENTIAL AND GOD-GIVEN DESTINY THROUGH INNER HEALING AND LIFE ADVANCEMENTS, BY GOING DEEPER AND GROWING HIGHER.

ANGELACRIST.ME

Barb Miller, author of *Kairos Time*, interior designer, coach, and speaker who helps women find beauty in the details of their life and home.

She founded ***Restoration Details,*** an interior design firm, in 2013. Soon after that, ***Life by Design Coaching*** was born, a program bringing inner beauty to women.

Barb loves all things beautiful and is passionate about teaching women how to create beauty—not only in their homes, but also in their lives. She will show you how to transform your life and create a radiance that is uniquely yours. Don't miss the Life changing journey the **GREAT DESIGNER** has for you. You're a one-of-a-kind masterpiece created for greatness and to be used for His glory!

Barb is wired to help people get **unstuck** and be **unstoppable** in every area of their life and home. She enjoys *helping* people, *inspiring* people, and *cheering* them on; it's not only her job, but also an undeniable calling from the Great Designer Himself. It is her privilege to walk alongside you in this life-transforming process called ***Life by Design*** where inner beauty is created.

Barb is married to Craig Miller, the love of her life, and they live in Ohio with their 13-year-old son, Jacob. They also have four grown children—Zachary, Phillip, Bridgette, and Nicolas—and are blessed with ten beautiful grandchildren.

You can find more life-changing programs on **RestorationRoyals.com**

DOING LIFE & HOME BY DESIGN
WITH BARB MILLER

GOD'S DESIGN
Kairos Time Coaching

INTERIOR DESIGN
Restoration Details

HOME BY DESIGN
Restoration Royals

SPEAKER    **COACH**    **SUBSCRIPTION COMMUNITY**

EMBRACE GOD'S DESIGN FOR YOUR HOME AND LIFE TODAY

RESTORATIONROYALS.COM

Niccie Kliegl, author of *The Legacy Series* and *Kairos Time*, coach, talk show host, and speaker is passionate about elevating others into their *sweet spot*.

She founded ***Fulfill Your Legacy***, her life and business coaching practice, in 2015 with a faith-based discipleship program that raises up Christian leaders who first get themself partnered with God, then bring God into their home, their community, and their nation. Niccie says, "Elevating others into their sweet spot where they get more out of life and work because they partner with God, know their divine purpose, and **Tap into the Trinity**© is what I'm meant to do!"

Niccie is most joyful over her **Legacy Leader** private community of individuals learning to **LIVE | LOVE | LEARN | LEAD according to the call God has on their life**. A big part of this is teaching other faith-based entrepreneurs how to start their own successful online businesses to which they have been called.

Niccie is married and lives in Iowa with her best friend and lover of 30 years, Jeff Kliegl. Together, they have two beautiful, grown daughters, Raya and Riley, and one sweet grandchild, Iris.

You can find out more about Niccie at nicciekliegl.com

LEGACY SERIES
WITH NICCIE KLIEGL

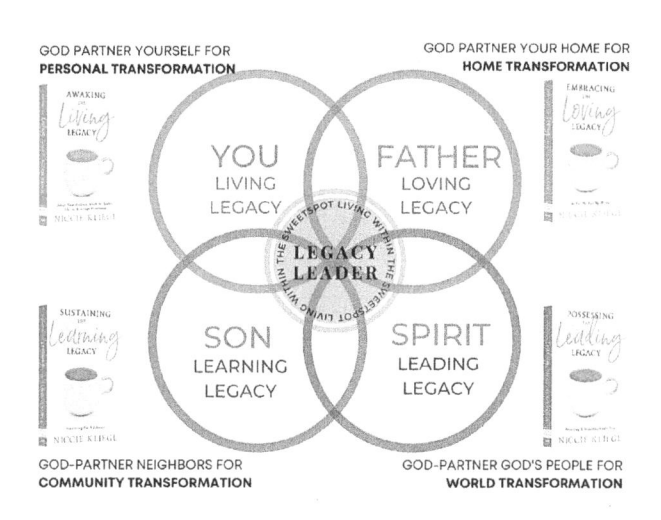

GOD PARTNER YOURSELF FOR
PERSONAL TRANSFORMATION

GOD PARTNER YOUR HOME FOR
HOME TRANSFORMATION

YOU — LIVING LEGACY
FATHER — LOVING LEGACY
SON — LEARNING LEGACY
SPIRIT — LEADING LEGACY

LEGACY LEADER

GOD-PARTNER NEIGHBORS FOR
COMMUNITY TRANSFORMATION

GOD-PARTNER GOD'S PEOPLE FOR
WORLD TRANSFORMATION

SPEAKER  **COACH**  **SUBSCRIPTION COMMUNITY**

START YOUR LIFE/HOME/COMMUNITY/NATION TRANSFORMATION TODAY

NICCIEKLIEGL.COM

Made in the USA
Monee, IL
29 November 2021